Annie Oakley

Legends of the Wild West

Sitting Bull

Billy the Kid

Calamity Jane

Buffalo Bill Cody

Crazy Horse

Davy Crockett

Wyatt Earp

Geronimo

Wild Bill Hickok

Jesse James

Nat Love

Annie Oakley

Legends of the Wild West

Annie Oakley

Rachel A. Koestler-Grack

CHELSEA HOUSE
PUBLISHERS
An imprint of Infobase Publishing

Annie Oakley

Copyright © 2010 by Infobase Publishing

Chelsea House
An imprint of Infobase Publishing
132 West 31st Street
New York NY 10001

Library of Congress Cataloging-in-Publication Data
Koestler-Grack, Rachel A., 1973-
  Annie Oakley / Rachel A. Koestler-Grack.
    p. cm. — (Legends of the Wild West)
  Includes bibliographical references and index.
  ISBN 978-1-60413-594-7 (hardcover)
  1. Oakley, Annie, 1860-1926--Juvenile literature. 2. Shooters of firearms—United States—Biography—Juvenile literature. 3. Entertainers—United States—Biography—Juvenile literature. 4. Women entertainers—United States—Biography—Juvenile literature. I. Title. II. Series.
  GV1157.O3K64 2010
  799.3'092—dc22
  [B]   2009041338

Text design by Kerry Casey
Cover design by Keith Trego
Composition by EJB Publishing Services
Cover printed by Bang Printing, Brainerd, Minn.
Book printed and bound by Bang Printing, Brainerd, Minn.
Date printed: March, 2010
Printed in the United States of America

10 9 8 7 6 5 4 3 2 1

CONTENTS

DEAD SHOT

At the center of the arena, 25-year-old Annie Oakley stood next to a table draped with a silk cloth. A row of rifles and shotguns lay across the tabletop. Nearby, Oakley's husband, Frank Butler, loaded the traps with clay birds. At first, he released one bird at a time. Oakley fired away, hitting each one. Then, he winged them in pairs, triplets, and finally, four at a time. No matter how many birds flew from the traps, Oakley shattered them all to pieces. Incredibly accurate and fast, she looked like a blur of motion. Yet, her shooting seemed almost effortless, as if her gun were simply an extension of her arm. Oftentimes, she shot with one hand resting casually on her hip. Also, she was ambidextrous, so she could fire just as well with her left hand as she could with her right. Sometimes, she took a pistol in each hand and fired them at the same time, smashing target after target.

Oakley saved her most difficult feat for last. The stunt required 1 rifle, 5 shotguns, 11 glass balls, and just 10 seconds on the clock. With the guns neatly lined up on the table, she began by lifting the rifle and turning it upside down. Butler tossed up one of the glass balls, and Oakley broke it with a shot from her upturned rifle. Next, with whirling speed, she picked up a shotgun. After unloading both barrels and shattering two more balls, she put the shotgun down and grabbed another. She continued to fire and smash balls, unloading all 5 shotguns, until she had broken all 11 glass balls—in

10 short ticks of a watch. After the last shot, Oakley carefully laid her smoking gun on the table. Playfully, she blew a kiss to the audience and skipped out of the arena.

From 1885 to 1913, Annie Oakley awed hundreds of thousands of people with her amazing shooting stunts. At the height of her career, she was the most famous woman in the United States. Some people even claimed she was the most famous woman in the world. Her legend began with Buffalo Bill's Wild West, an outdoor western show that later would inspire movies and television shows. The Wild West debuted in 1883. The show was a combination of rodeo stunts and drama skits. Buffalo Bill wanted audiences to feel as though they were getting a snapshot of the real American West. He hired genuine cowboys and true Native Americans, mostly Pawnee and Sioux. The show featured animals, including buffalo, elk, mountain sheep, and hundreds of horses. Buffalo Bill's Wild West was completely authentic, right down to the Deadwood stagecoach, which was used in a robbery skit. Years earlier, this same coach had made the run between Cheyenne, Wyoming, and Deadwood, South Dakota. In other acts, cowboys rode bucking broncos and lassoed buffalo. Native Americans pounded drums and went on the warpath. At one point in the show, a Pony Express rider changed horses while galloping along at lightning speed. And of course, Annie Oakley blasted glass balls out of the air and turned tiny marbles into puffs of dust.

For 17 years, Oakley performed in the Wild West arena as a dead shot sharpshooter. Her skills were unmatched by any female shooter and most male shooters of her time. One of her most famous feats involved the ace of hearts playing card. Using a .22 caliber rifle from a distance of 90 feet (27 meters), she could split the edge of the card and pierce it with five more bullet holes before it dropped to the ground.

Most people think of Oakley as only an exhibition shooter, or a show shooter. In truth, she preferred a much different type of shooting. She was a sportsman at heart. She preferred the woods to dusty arena tents. She loved the hunter's life—rising at the first sliver of

Annie Oakley, born as Phoebe Ann Moses (or Mosey), was a superstar sharp-shooter at a time when only men carried guns and knew how to shoot them. Oakley won dozens of medals (as shown pinned to her dress), fame, and fortune, and continued to set shooting records into her sixties.

dawn, trampling through forests with her dogs, the sound of crackling leaves under her boots, and the smell of burnt gunpowder. She wished more women shared her love of hunting. "Any woman who does not thoroughly enjoy tramping across the country on a clear frosty morning with a good gun and a pair of dogs does not know how to enjoy life," she once said, as quoted in *Annie Oakley* by Shirl Kasper.

Her exhibition shooting paid the bills, though. In fact, her spot in the arena paid quite well, although Oakley would never admit it. At a time when the average worker in the United States made less than $500 a year, Oakley made about $150 a week. However, she never forgot what it was like to be poor. At a very early age, she had learned to skimp and save. Even when she and Butler became wealthy, she was always frugal. Once, she got talked into a game of penny-ante poker. She lost about 80 cents in the game. For weeks, she complained about her "heavy losses," and she could never be coaxed into another game again.

TRUE WESTERNER

In her lifetime and throughout history, Oakley became a symbol of what Americans value most. Her character was rooted in hard work, simplicity, modesty, ambition, kindness, generosity, perseverance, and a love of animals and nature. People admired Oakley's genuine personality. She held firm to her integrity, both as a performer and as a person. She always demanded honest applause for her stunts, and she stood up for herself whenever her good name was in danger of being tarnished.

Her role as part of the classic American West only grew larger after her death in 1926. Her real-life story represented the life of a true westerner: She came from humble beginnings, a poor girl on the Ohio frontier. She learned how to handle a gun and used it to make a living for herself. She was independent and fearless, galloping on what was considered a man's territory. Yet, she somehow remained a feminine and respectable lady.

Annie Oakley received top billing and appeared on posters for Buffalo Bill's Wild West show. She became America's first female superstar.

A few months before her death, a famous cowboy wrote an article about her in which he described her life. "It is a good story about a little woman that all the older generation remember," the cowboy, Will Rogers, wrote, as it appears in *The Colonel and Little Missie: Buffalo Bill, Annie Oakley, and the Beginnings of Superstardom in America*. "She was the reigning sensation of America and Europe during all the heyday of Buffalo Bill's Wild West show. She was their star. Her picture was on more billboards than a modern Gloria Swanson [the 1920s movie star]. It was Annie Oakley, the greatest woman rifle shot the world has ever produced. Nobody took her place. There was only one."

POOR BEGINNINGS

Greenville in Darke County, Ohio, was once an area of lush, thick forest that stretched for miles. It was here that General Anthony Wayne built a pioneer fort called Fort Greene Ville, the largest wooden fortification ever built. General Wayne, also called Mad Anthony, led the victory at the Battle of Fallen Timbers in 1794, a battle between the United States and the American Indian tribes of the Western Confederacy for control of the Northwest Territory. This territory included the land west of Pennsylvania and northwest of the Ohio River, making up the modern states of Ohio, Indiana, Illinois, Michigan, and Wisconsin, and the northeastern part of Minnesota. The victory over the Western Confederacy, one of the strongest alliances among American Indian tribes to date, and the subsequent signing of the Treaty of Greenville, paved the way for the creation of the state of Ohio in 1803. White settlers arrived in droves after that, clearing the forests to plant corn and graze cows.

Hardworking men like Jacob Moses were the ones who had come to make a living on the land. Jacob and his wife, Susan, had moved to the woodlands of Darke County and settled in a little village called Woodland. This tiny settlement would later have a buggy shop, an ice house, a saloon, a restaurant, and a cream station, but at the time the Moseses moved there, it did not even have a general store.

Jacob and Susan, Quakers from Hollidaysburg, Pennsylvania, had come to Darke County sometime between the birth of their daughters Elizabeth in 1855 and Sarah Ellen in 1857. The Moseses had moved to a rented farm in order to make a fresh start after their tavern in Hollidaysburg had burned down. In a crude log cabin on the farm, on August 13, 1860, the fifth of their seven children was born. They named her Phoebe Ann.

Phoebe's sisters gave her the nickname Annie. She was a beautiful girl with thick, coffee-colored hair and striking blue-gray eyes. Although she was small, she was far from dainty. Annie took no interest in her sisters' ragdolls. Instead, she became somewhat of a tomboy, spending most of her time with her father and younger brother John.

In the 1860s, Ohio was part of the wild frontier, and the entire Moses family had to work hard to survive. All of the children were expected to pitch in and help with chores. They built fences around their farm, tanned cowhide to make their own shoes, smoked ham, pickled beans, and picked apples. Annie spent many afternoons wandering through the forests gathering hickory nuts, walnuts, and wild cherries. After her father taught her to how to make traps out of cornstalks, Annie trapped quail and rabbit for family meals.

FAMILY TRAGEDY

On a snowy night in 1866, life changed for Annie and her family. One winter morning, Jacob Moses loaded his wagon with corn and wheat, hitched up the horses, and set out for the nearest mill, 14 miles (22.5 kilometers) away. He was gone all day, and before he returned, a blizzard arose. Midnight came and passed, and still there was no sign of Jacob. From time to time, Susan anxiously peered out the window, praying to catch a glimpse of her husband's wagon through the whirling snow. At last, the whine of wagon wheels could be heard outside the cabin. Susan threw open the door and rushed out into the freezing wind. Outside, Jacob sat stiff as an icicle in the buckboard seat. The reins were crusted with ice and frozen to his wrists. He was too cold even to speak. As soon as the winds died down, Susan fetched the doctor, but it was too late. Jacob had suffered severe frostbite, which caused his strong and sturdy body to become weak and frail. In the weeks that followed, he became sick with pneumonia. That March, he died.

Annie's family was left destitute, without any money or support. Taking care of the farm was too much for the young family to handle. They moved out of their home and rented a smaller, run-down house, but life did not improve. Not long after, Annie's oldest sister, Mary Jane, became sick with tuberculosis and died. Susan was forced to sell the family cow—named Pink—to pay doctor and funeral bills. Susan found work as a maternity nurse but was still unable to care for all of her children. She had to take drastic steps, agreeing to let another family, the Bartholomews, adopt her youngest girl, Hulda.

LIFE WITH THE WOLVES

Finally, in 1870, Susan had to let 10-year-old Annie go, too. She sent Annie to the poor farm, a county-sponsored farm that housed and cared for the poor and orphaned. The poor farm, or the Infirmary as the locals called it, was a three-story brick building that spanned the Greenville and Easton pikes, located just two-and-a-half miles (four km) from Greenville. Before Annie could even get settled in there, a local farmer came by the poor farm to look for a girl to help his wife with chores and the care of their newborn baby. In those days, poor farms often rented out children as servants or farmhands. In her autobiography, Annie never gave the name of this family, but she called them "the Wolves." They were cruel and treated her like a slave. Each day, the farmer woke her up at 4:00 in the morning, and from that moment on, she worked almost nonstop until evening. She made breakfast, milked the cows, washed dishes, skimmed milk, fed the calves and pigs, pumped water for the cattle, fed the chickens, rocked the baby to sleep, weeded the garden, picked wild blackberries, and got dinner ready.

One day, Annie received a letter from her mother, asking her to come home. The farmer and his wife, however, would not let her

Poor farms were common in the United States and in Europe from the mid-nineteenth century until about 1950. The farms were supported at public expense, and residents (the poor and the elderly) worked for their room and board by laboring in the fields and providing care for other residents. Pictured is the poor farm where Annie Oakley lived for several years.

leave. "I was held a prisoner," Annie later wrote, as recorded in *Annie Oakley* by Shirl Kasper. Sometimes, the Wolves even abused her, although Annie never told anyone much about those painful experiences. In her autobiography, she casually mentioned that there were times she had scars and welts on her back. Annie also described a night when the farmer's wife threw her out into the icy snow because she had fallen asleep while doing some darning. Barefoot and shivering, Annie might have died if the farmer had not come home and let her inside.

Finally, in 1872, Annie decided she had taken enough abuse. One spring day, she had an opportunity to escape. The family left for the day, and Annie stayed at the house to iron a huge basket of clothes. "Suddenly I thought, why not run away," she later wrote, as quoted in *The Life and Legacy of Annie Oakley*. She bundled her few belongings into a cloth wrap and ran to the railroad station. But she had only 48 cents, not enough for a ticket to Greenville. At the station, she told a kind gentleman all about her dreadful life with the Wolves and said that she was running away. Pitying poor Annie, the man offered to pay her passage back to the poor farm.

Annie went to live with the new superintendent at the poor farm, Samuel Crawford Edington, and his wife, Nancy Ann, who were friends of Annie's mother. They treated her like a daughter and gave her a comfortable, loving home. Annie quickly made friends with the Edingtons' children, and she began to attend school with them. The Edingtons soon saw that Annie was a talented, responsible young lady. They began to pay her to work as a seamstress, sewing dresses and quilts for the children at the poor farm. She also learned to embroider and stitched fancy designs on the cuffs and collars of the orphans' shabby dresses. Eventually, the Edingtons also hired her to take care of the dairy. She milked the 12 cows, skimmed off the cream, and churned butter for the poor farm's kitchen. Annie earned a raise, and always one to think ahead, she saved her money.

While Annie was away, her mother had married Daniel Brumbaugh. Soon after their marriage, he died, leaving Susan alone again and with a newborn baby named Emily. When Annie was about 15 years old, her mother got married a third time, to a widower named Joseph Shaw. Susan and her new husband built a house in North Star, not far from Woodland, Ohio. Finally, Susan could afford to care for her children. She wrote to Annie and invited her back home.

GIRL WITH A GUN

As Annie left Greenville, she started to draw plans for her future. Before leaving town, she dropped by the Katzenberger brothers'

Poor Farms

Poor farms, sometimes called poorhouses, were common in the 1800s. Much like present-day homeless shelters, the poor farms supported and housed needy people of all ages. Able-bodied residents were expected to do chores, help care for other residents, or work in the grain fields. The number of poor farms began to decline after the Social Security Act was passed in 1935. The act offered federal aid to the poor and disabled, including housing assistance and food stamps. By 1950, poor farms had almost completely disappeared.

Oakley never forgot her years at the poor farm, even after she became a famous fancy shooter. In 1913, she performed her stunts in Greenville, Ohio, as part of the Young Buffalo Wild West show. She gave free tickets to all the orphan children at the Darke County Children's Home, so they could come see her act. She also served free ice cream and treats to the children there. Years later, she even paid for a number of orphan girls to receive a high school education.

grocery store at the corner of Main Street and the town square. Annie had been there many times before, running errands for the Edingtons. The Katzenberger brothers—G. Anthony and Charles— often accepted trades from hunters and trappers. Men brought in their wild turkeys and rabbits in exchange for flour, wheat, and ammunition. When Annie was younger—before she went to the poor farm—she used to trade her kills with the Katzenbergers. Annie tried to strike a business deal with the brothers. She told them she was going home to the north county woods to hunt and to trap. She wondered if the Katzenbergers would buy any small game if she sent it to Greenville. The brothers agreed. From that day on, Annie would earn a living with her sure aim and a gun.

Most people at that time would have thought a girl with a gun was a strange sight. In those days, girls were not supposed to shoot guns; it wasn't ladylike. But Annie was hooked. As Kasper writes in *Annie Oakley*, "'My mother . . . was perfectly horrified when I began shooting and tried to keep me in school,' Annie said, 'but I would run away and go quail shooting in the woods.'" Annie wasn't a typical girl. In fact, she already felt quite comfortable with a gun. By the time she was about eight years old, Annie had grown tired of trapping quails and rabbit. She was eager to learn how to shoot. Day after day, she would stare up at her father's old, forbidden Kentucky rifle that hung over the fireplace. She longed to lift it off the rack and wrap her finger around the trigger, but she was not allowed. One day, Annie just could not fight the urge, and she climbed up on a chair and slid the rifle down off the mantel.

Eight-year-old Annie took her first shot that afternoon. She saw a squirrel run down the grassy hill in front of her house and leap onto the fence to snatch a hickory nut. Annie lifted up the heavy barrel and rested it on the porch railing, took aim, and fired. "It was a wonderful shot, going right through the head from side to side," she recalled in *Annie Oakley*. "I still consider it one of the best shots I ever made."

That shot may have tickled Annie, but not everyone was as thrilled as she was. Her brother John was so angry she used the rifle that he quickly thought up a plan to teach her a lesson. He secretly put a double load of ammo in his shotgun and handed the gun to Annie, taunting her to try another shot. He figured the jolting kick she would get when she fired it would be enough to discourage her from ever shooting again. He tossed his hat into the air as a target. To his surprise, Annie not only handled the kickback just fine, but she also made a mess of his hat. After just two shots, it was painfully clear—at least to John—that Annie had a special talent when it came to shooting guns.

Back home with her mother, 15-year-old Annie studied hunting techniques and the nature of certain prey, set traps, and hunted. She learned all the tricks of the trade—rabbits hid in the hedgerows, grouse in wooded gullies and ravines, and quail in the stalky stubble of the fields. When the birds took off from their hiding places, they swooped up so fast she could hardly catch a glimpse of them. Her aim had to be precise, fired on pure intuition. The challenge thrilled her. She never shot at sitting game, as many hunters did. "I always preferred taking my shot when the game was on the move," she said, as quoted in *Annie Oakley*. "It gave them a fair chance, and made me quick of eye and hand."

Dressed in a short skirt and knickerbockers (baggy pants that come to the knee), long stockings, and copper-toed boots, Annie was an odd sight in the wild woods and dusty fields. Still, it was where she felt most at home. She loved the crunch of leaves under her feet and the smell of burnt gunpowder in the air. "I guess the love of a gun must have been born in me," Annie once said (in *Annie Oakley*). For Annie, shooting a gun was as easy as pointing her finger. The gun was more like a natural extension of her arm. "You must have your mind, your nerve and everything in harmony," she once advised. "Don't look at your gun, simply follow the object with the end of it, as if the tip of the barrel was the point of your finger."

When Annie was 16 years old, she got what she called her first "real gun"—a Parker Brothers 16-gauge breech-loading hammer. The latest in firearms, a breech-loading shotgun allowed the shooter to load the shells at home and later just slip them into the barrel when out hunting. It was much more convenient than Annie's old muzzle-loader, which required her to carry a powder horn and ramrod. Also, it allowed Annie to hunt on any day—rain or shine. With her muzzle-loader, the powder often got wet on rainy days and failed to ignite.

Her new gun at her side, Annie shot more game than ever. She tied them in bunches of 6 and 12 and shipped them by mail coach to the Katzenbergers' store. From there, the Katzenbergers sold the game to hotels in Cincinnati, which was only 80 miles (129 km) from Greenville. According to legend, the hotelkeepers preferred the quail and rabbits that Annie killed because they were always shot through the head. For this reason, there were never any worries about guests finding buckshot in their dinners. Naturally, the Katzenberger brothers grew quite fond of their sharpshooter. One Christmas, they sent Annie a special present: a can of DuPont Eagle Ducking Black

Powder, five pounds of shot, and two boxes of percussion caps. Annie was especially excited about the high-grade DuPont powder. Sure she would never again own another can of such good powder, days went by before she could bring herself to break the seal and use it.

Annie's skills as a market hunter gave her a reasonable income. In those days, conserving the environment was not yet a public issue, and there were no limits on how much game someone could shoot. For example, around the Great Lakes, a skilled hunter could kill up to 200 deer in a single autumn. At $15 to $20 apiece, the hunter could make more money in one season than the average lumberjack or miner could earn in an entire year. Annie made enough money shooting at small game to pay off the $200 mortgage on her mother's house.

Annie's popularity as a sure shot spread throughout North Star. By the time Annie was 18,

Annie Oakley learned to shoot a gun when she was just eight years old, and by age nine she was supporting her family and widowed mother with the game that she caught. By the time she was 15, Oakley was a skilled sharpshooter with a successful hunting business.

she had won so many local turkey shoots—a popular form of entertainment at the time—that she was barred from entering them. As it turned out, though, something much more rewarding was waiting around the bend. Her local reputation led her to a shooting match that would change the course of her life.

"LITTLE SURE SHOT"

While Annie Moses was growing up in Ohio, Americans all over the country were talking about some other impressive shooters. In 1869, when Annie was nine years old, Captain Adam H. Bogardus became famous by killing 100 pigeons without missing a single one. That same year, he made a $1,000 bet that he could kill 500 pigeons in 645 minutes (10 hours and 45 minutes). The captain easily won his cash, with 117 minutes to spare (just under 2 hours). In 1871, Bogardus became a national champion sharpshooter. By the time Annie was 15 years old, Bogardus had been crowned champion of the world. In the 1870s and 1880s, America boasted dozens of sharpshooters, though. Captain Bogardus was just the most famous of these exhibition shooters—or shooters who performed fancy stunts with their guns.

Bogardus's biggest rival was Doc Carver, who tried to knock the captain off his throne in the summer of 1878. One sunny morning, Carver showed up at Deerfoot Park in New York City all decked out in western attire. He wore a broad sombrero cocked on his head and a velvet shirt with a silk scarf tied around his neck. His pantaloons were tucked inside his boots, and as he walked, the sunlight bounced off his huge, golden belt buckle in blinding bursts. With his long, wily hair and a glistening Winchester rifle hanging at his side, he was a menacing sight. His plans were equally serious. He had promised quite a show for the spectators. He was going to break 5,500 glass balls in 500 minutes (8 hours and 20 minutes), a feat that had never been tried before.

Carver took his place on a small hill, surrounded by barrels of feather-filled glass balls and boxes of cartridges. At exactly 11:00, Carver's assistant, Horace Fletcher, grabbed a glass ball from a barrel and tossed it into the air. Moments later, Carver fired his rifle, shattering the glass and sending bits of feathers floating to the ground. As fast as he could, Fletcher threw one ball after another. One by one, Carver shot them down. Before long, feathers littered the sky like snowflakes in a winter storm.

As soon as Carver emptied one gun, Fletcher handed him another. By early evening, Carver's buckskin gloves were black with gunpowder. His face was beaded with perspiration, and his eyes were swollen and bloodshot from dusty smoke, glass grits, and feather fuzz. At last, he shouted, "For God's sake boys, how much more have I got to do?" Fletcher called back, as written in *Annie Oakley*, "Just 100 more, and 18 minutes to do them in." At the end of the day, Carver made his quota. He hit 5,500 out of 6,208 and still had 10 minutes to spare.

In the years that followed, other shooters staged various other feats. Women soon entered the arena, as well. One day in 1880, sharpshooter John Ruth surprised spectators when he handed his wife a pistol during his exhibition. He tossed a glass ball into the air, and she took aim and blasted it into shards. Mrs. Ruth proved that a woman could handle a gun just as well as a man. She performed many tricky stunts. She shattered glass balls while holding her pistol sideways and upside down. On occasion, she even turned her back toward the target and took aim using a small mirror. To make the feat harder, her target was a swinging ball.

By this time, an Irish immigrant named Frank Butler had opened a shooting act in New York City. Butler and his partner, a man known only by the name of Baughman, heralded themselves as champion marksmen. When the show did not take off, however,

Traveling show marksman Frank Butler lost a shooting match to Annie Oakley but won her heart. He went on to marry her, one of the best decisions of both his personal and professional life.

they joined the Sells Brothers Circus, performing their shooting act under the big top. They shattered glass balls, shot backward while sighting in a mirror, and knocked apples off each other's heads from 15 paces apart. Through Sells Brothers, Butler and Baughman's popularity grew, and they soon became known as the "Champion Rifle Dead-Shots of the World."

In April 1881, Baughman and Butler visited Cincinnati, Ohio. At their hotel, Butler met some farmers who dangled in front of them a tantalizing wager. The farmers said they knew a shooter from Greenville who would challenge the marksman, and they bet $100 that this mystery shooter could beat him. Butler found it hard not to laugh at the farmers' suggestion. Greenville was 80 miles (129 km) out of Butler's way, but he could not resist the easy money. "I thought there were some country people who thought someone could shoot a little and were ready to lose money," Butler later said in *Annie Oakley*, "and as I needed it, I went out."

BUTLER MEETS HIS MATCH

A spring storm had dumped 28 inches (71 centimeters) of snow in Greenville the day before the match, but nothing could weigh down Butler's spirits as he arrived in town. He had bragged that he could outshoot anyone, except perhaps Carver and Bogardus. Certainly, he would have no trouble whipping this unknown shooter. The match took place about 18 miles (29 km) outside of Greenville. There, Butler waited to meet his contender.

When he saw Annie approaching, he asked someone nearby the identity of this pretty country girl. The spectator told him that she was his opponent. Butler took another look at Annie and burst out laughing. Annie, however, quickly wiped the smile from his face. Wearing a calf-length skirt and a stern expression, she stepped up to the mark. Butler won the coin toss, so he took the first shot. He called out "pull," and the referee opened the trap, releasing a clay bird into the sky. Butler fired, hitting his target, and the referee announced it "dead." Then, Annie lifted her gun, shouted "pull," and repeated the stunt. Pull after pull, their scores stayed tied up, until Butler missed a shot. He had 24 hits. If Annie nailed her next bird, she would win the match. She took a deep breath and lined up her gun. As the clay bird soared higher, she carefully aimed and pulled the trigger. A few silent moments ticked by. Then, the broken target hit the ground with sprinkling thuds, "dead." Annie had beaten Butler, 25 to 24.

Butler was curiously impressed with this young shooter. "Never were the birds so hard for two shooters as they flew from us, but never did a person make more impossible shots than did that little girl," he said, as quoted in *Annie Oakley*. "It was her first big match—my first defeat." He walked Annie back to her carriage and handed her several passes to his show. Annie agreed to go see his act in Cincinnati.

At the show, Annie was more impressed with Butler's poodle, George, than she was with his shooting skills. George, who normally was not fond of women, instantly liked Annie. At one point in the act, Butler shot an apple off George's head. George picked up a chunk of the apple with his mouth, trotted over to Annie, and dropped it at her feet. Days later, Annie sent a letter to George. In response, Butler had a box of candy delivered to her, from George. Through George, Annie and Butler started a romantic relationship that quickly blossomed into love. They were married on June 20, 1882, in Windsor, Ontario, Canada (some accounts give their wedding date as August 23, 1876). Annie never forgot the little poodle that played matchmaker. "Well, what fools we mortals be!" Annie later wrote, as recorded in *The Life and Legacy of Annie Oakley*. "If that poodle didn't lead me into signing [marriage papers] . . . that tied a knot so hard it has lasted some 50 years."

Although Butler was 10 years older than Annie, he was an excellent choice. In Frank Butler, Annie found a husband, friend, shooting partner, business manager, and agent. With his experience, he could train Annie to be one of the greatest fancy shooters ever to hit the stage.

Sometime in late 1882 or early 1883, Butler's new stage partner, John Graham, became ill. Butler asked Annie to step in as Graham's replacement, holding the objects as he shot. To build up the suspense, Butler often missed his first shot or two on purpose. One day, however, he could not hit his mark. He missed over and over again, about a dozen times, while Annie stood patiently holding the target. A man in the crowd shouted, "Let the girl shoot," as recorded in *Annie Oakley*. Butler handed Annie the gun. She fired and hit the target on her second try, even though she had never practiced the shot. The crowd roared with cheers, and when Butler tried to resume his act, they booed him. That day, Annie finished the show.

Butler knew a good act when he saw one. From that day on, Annie was his new partner. She chose the stage name Annie Oakley, and the new show advertised the shooting team of Butler and Oakley. How Annie came up with the name Oakley is unknown. It may have been a family name; others say she took it from the Oakley neighborhood of Cincinnati. Or she may have just come up with it out of the blue. Using the skills she learned at the poor farm, Oakley designed and sewed her own costume: an ankle-length dress with pretty, embroidered cuffs. At first, spectators probably had their doubts about this petite, 5-foot, 110-pound (152-centimeter, 50-kilogram) young lady as she lined up on stage. During the performance, Butler would shoot first, and Oakley would repeat the shot. George the poodle also grabbed his share of the spotlight. Butler would place an apple on his head, and Oakley would split it with a bullet. Then, George would snatch a piece of the apple out of the air and gobble it up.

For a little over a year, Butler and Oakley traveled throughout the Midwest and along the Great Lakes. They performed their act at variety theaters and skating rinks, living off whatever money they could muster from ticket sales. Then, they signed a 40-week contract with the Sells Brothers Circus in Columbus, Ohio, to begin in April 1884. They would finish out their bookings and head for Columbus. One of those final acts took place at the Olympic Theatre in St. Paul, Minnesota. That day became one of the most talked about moments of Annie Oakley's life.

On March 19, 1884, Butler and Oakley prepared for their act like any other time. This evening, though, a distinguished guest sat

Sitting Bull

Born about 1831, Sitting Bull was a member of the Hunkpapa band of the Lakota Sioux. This nomadic American Indian group lived on the grassy plains of present-day North Dakota, South Dakota, and Montana, as well as areas of Wyoming. At age 21, Sitting Bull became a member of the Strong Hearts. This group of warriors showed impressive bravery and battle skills during wars against enemy tribes. Few warriors earned this honor. In 1856, during a battle against the Crow tribe, Sitting Bull killed the Crow chief. For this courageous act, he was named a member of the Midnight Strong Heart Society. Only the most valiant Lakota were allowed into this group. During that same year, Sitting Bull also became a holy man, called a *wichasha wakan*. As a holy man, he often spoke to the Great Spirit, a sacred Lakota spirit, who gave him visions of future events.

In 1857, Sitting Bull became a war chief of the Hunkpapa. In the late 1860s, he was named the head chief of the Lakota nation. Sitting Bull is most famous for his role in the major victory at the Battle of Little Bighorn against Lieutenant Colonel George Armstrong Custer and his army. For years, the Lakota had struggled to keep white settlers off their land. Despite promises to stop invading Lakota territory, the U.S. Army and white settlers continued to push onto their homeland. Finally, the Lakota Sioux had no other choice but to battle the U.S. Army.

in the crowd. The Lakota Sioux chief, Sitting Bull, had gone to the Olympic Theatre on Seventh Street to see the Arlington and Fields Combination, a variety of acts that included the Wertz brothers as acrobats, singer Miss Allie Jackson, and Butler and Oakley. Sitting Bull was a captured American Indian, who had been blamed for the death of Lieutenant Colonel George Armstrong Custer at the Battle of Little Bighorn eight years earlier.

Oakley playfully skipped on stage, lifted her rifle, and aimed the barrel at a burning candle. In one shot, she snuffed out the flame

Sitting Bull had a vision that his warriors would defeat the U.S. soldiers in a great battle. In his vision, he saw an army of soldiers falling from the sky with their heads bowed and their hats tumbling down. On June 25, 1876, Sitting Bull's vision came true. The Lakota defeated Custer and his cavalry of soldiers on the grassy hills near the Little Bighorn River in present-day Montana. During the fight, Custer and 210 soldiers were killed. In the months after the battle, Sitting Bull fled the United States to Wood Mountain, Saskatchewan, Canada, where he stayed until 1881. He then surrendered to American forces and spent two years as a prisoner at Fort Randall. In 1883, the U.S. government let Sitting Bull join his relatives and friends at the Standing Rock Reservation in South Dakota.

In 1885, Sitting Bull joined Buffalo Bill's Wild West show. He toured the United States with this western theater production, which featured the shooting stunts of Annie Oakley. After touring with the show, Sitting Bull returned to the Standing Rock Reservation. Around this time, the U.S. government planned to separate the reservation into six smaller reservations as part of the Sioux Act of 1889. Each Lakota would receive a portion of the land, and the rest would be sold to settlers. Sitting Bull opposed this separation of the Sioux tribe. Afraid Sitting Bull might lead an uprising, U.S. army officials ordered his arrest. When the officers came to apprehend Sitting Bull on December 15, 1890, members of his tribe tried to stop them. During the struggle, Sitting Bull was shot dead.

with a whizzing bullet. Sitting Bull watched her knock corks off of bottles and slice through a cigar Butler held in his teeth. He was amazed by the stunts this tiny woman could perform. Later that week, Sitting Bull sent Oakley $65 along with a letter asking to buy an autographed photo of her. Amused, Oakley offered him a signed picture, but returned the money with it.

The next day, she called on Sitting Bull. He was so delighted that he insisted on adopting her as a tribal daughter. He called her "Watanya Cicilla," or "Little Sure Shot." Of course, the adoption

Annie Oakley's marksmanship so impressed Sitting Bull, political and spiritual chief of the Lakota Sioux, that he offered $65 for a photograph of her. Adopting her as his tribal daughter, Sitting Bull gave her the tribal name "Watanya Cicilla," or "Little Sure Shot."

was not formal. However, Sitting Bull told her that, if she ever decided to live in Indian Territory, she would be entitled to receive five ponies, a wigwam, endless cattle, and other presents as the chief's daughter.

Butler saw the story as a great piece of advertising. Just two weeks later, he placed an ad in the *New York Clipper* that read: "The Premier Shots, Butler and Oakley, Captured by Sitting Bull." After their meeting, Sitting Bull and Oakley parted ways. He headed west to the Standing Rock Reservation, while she went east to Ohio. But their paths would cross again someday.

JOINING
THE WILD WEST

Between the 1840s and the 1880s, circuses provided an affordable family show throughout the Midwest. The Sells Brothers Circus was one of the most famous, advertised as "a whole world of wonders," "greater than the greatest," and "better than the best." Sells boasted 50 cages of live wild animals, including the biggest hippopotamuses, the tallest and only full-grown giraffe, a two-horned rhinoceros, and a huge arctic aquarium swirling with water beasts. The star of the show was Emperor, a giant elephant. During his act, he led 10 teams of elephants pulling 10 golden chariots.

Most circuses also featured shooting acts, like Butler and Oakley. The couple, however, was not a headlining act. Crowds flocked to the big top mostly to see the animals and acrobatic stunts. By the end of the 1884 season, Oakley would perform in front of packed crowds in 187 cities in 13 states, including Arkansas, Illinois, Kansas, Missouri, Ohio, and Texas. Still, she was not nearly as famous as Emperor the elephant. On tour, Annie also performed in a pantomime act, which starred Humpty Dumpty the clown and Old One-Two the pantaloon (a foolish old man who is the target of a clown's jokes). In this silent comedy routine, Oakley played Mrs. Old One-Two and Butler was a character named Quaker Starchback.

In the late 1800s, the Sells Brothers Circus was one of the largest and most successful shows in the country. At its height, the show was transported from town to town using 47 special railroad cars. The Sells Brothers eventually became part of the Ringling Brothers and Barnum and Bailey circus.

The circus may have glittered for spectators, but it was far from glamorous for the performers. Bookings were sporadic, and paychecks could not be counted on. On the road, they barely got enough food to survive, and their sleeping quarters would not have even been fit for the animals. On more than one occasion during the tour, Oakley complained about the conditions. She especially raised a ruckus when her saddle became unsafe for riding.

In December, the Sells Brothers Circus headed for New Orleans. The crew would finish up the 1884 season at the World's Industrial and Cotton Exposition, hoping to cash in on the thousands of visitors in town for the expo. The circus performed every day, but the crowds were scarce due to rainy weather. Constant downpours forced the circus to pack up and head back to Ohio after only two weeks. The next season would not start until the following April. Unless Butler and Oakley could book some shows on their own, they were out of work—at least for the winter.

Butler had hoped to revive their variety show and tour until the circus reopened in the spring. Then, on December 4, he read in the local paper that Buffalo Bill's Wild West show would soon be setting up right off Canal Street, not far from the Sells Brothers' lot. William F. Cody, better known as Buffalo Bill, was scheduled to arrive in New Orleans in just a few days. According to rumors, Cody planned to run his show through the entire winter. Perhaps Cody would hire Butler and Oakley. Cody arrived in New Orleans on December 8—just in the nick of time. The Sells' circus planned to close on December 13.

Sometime during that week, Butler and Oakley visited the Wild West lot to introduce themselves to Buffalo Bill. They asked him for a job, but much to their disappointment, Cody had nothing to offer them. His show was already booked solid with shooting acts, including the famous Captain Bogardus. So, with the chance of a job seemingly gone, Oakley and Butler packed their bags and headed north.

Meanwhile, Buffalo Bill's show went on in New Orleans without them. However, it turned out to be a tough winter for the Wild West.

Buffalo Bill

William "Buffalo Bill" Cody was born near Le Claire, Iowa, on February 26, 1846. At age 12, he left home and went to work for a wagon train on its way to Fort Laramie, Wyoming. The following year, he went to California hoping to find a fortune in the Gold Rush. At age 15, he became a Pony Express rider, carrying mail from Missouri to California on horseback. He served as a scout for the Union Army during the Civil War and later years,

(continues)

Buffalo Bill Cody, one of the most famous showmen of the Old West.

(continued)

earning the Congressional Medal of Honor for his service during the Indian Wars of the 1870s. Three weeks after the Battle of Little Bighorn, Cody's
scouting regiment attacked a group of Cheyenne warriors. During the fight,
Cody killed and scalped a warrior named Yellow Hair.

In 1867, Cody began to hunt buffalo and quickly picked up the nickname "Buffalo Bill" for his expert shooting. In 1883, he created Buffalo Bill's
Wild West, which brought him worldwide fame. His amazing sharpshoot-
ers, trick riders, and western skits attracted huge crowds. For 30 years, he
brought the spirit of the Wild West to people around the world. He died of
kidney failure on January 10, 1917. In a heartfelt tribute to the man who
had made her a legend, Oakley called Cody "the kindest, simplest, most
loyal man I ever knew . . . the personification of those sturdy and lovable
qualities that really made the West."

Troubles began when the steamship carrying the show's sets and
equipment, including the animals, collided with another steamer
on the Mississippi River and sank. Captain Bogardus left at once
for Cincinnati to try to find the owners of the steamboat and collect
money for his lost possessions. In New Orleans, Cody had trouble
reorganizing the show without his star performer. To make matters
worse, the weather that winter continued to be miserable. Heavy
showers flooded the streets and turned the lot off Canal Street into
a soupy mud hole.

On March 9, 1885, Bogardus was so disgusted with the situation that he quit the show. Without Bogardus, Cody was forced to
do more shooting stunts himself. Discouraged, he even considered
closing the show for good. When Butler and Oakley heard about
Cody's dreadful predicament, they saw a golden opportunity. Oakley wrote to Buffalo Bill right away and asked for a spot in the program. Cody, however, thought the salary she requested was much
too steep. Oakley never revealed the salary she proposed, but it
was probably at least five times what the Wild West cowboys were

making. With the show struggling for survival, Cody was hesitant to sign such an expensive act.

In addition, Cody worried that little Oakley might not have the physical strength to do the job. Bogardus's shotguns weighed 10 pounds (4.5 kg) each. Cody just could not see a tiny 110-pound (50-kg) woman holding up that kind of weight day after day, show after show. "At first, Colonel Cody entertained a grave doubt as to whether I should be able to withstand the recoil from a shotgun," Oakley said, as quoted in *Annie Oakley* by Shirl Kasper. By this time, there were many more fancy shooters on the stage, all of whom used pistols and rifles. In fact, Oakley's unique edge as a woman shooter had grown dangerously thin. But no one had ever heard of a female exhibition shooter who used a shotgun. She would have to be as good as Captain Bogardus, shattering glass balls and clay pigeons in midair. These stunts were quite a bit more difficult than shooting corks and bottles on the variety stage.

Still, Oakley was always confident when it came to a gun. To prove she would be worth every penny of that salary, she agreed to a three-day trial. If Cody was not satisfied, she would leave the show, no questions asked. Cody liked the deal and invited her to join the Wild West in Louisville, Kentucky, where the show was to open a new season at the end of April.

STAR PERFORMER

In April 1885, Butler and Oakley took off for Kentucky and never looked back. They brought along their beloved poodle, George. Oakley felt confident about her audition. Before she left Cincinnati, she had attempted the greatest endurance feat of her life. With three 16-gauge Park shotguns, she tried to break 5,000 glass balls in one day—just as Doc Carver and Captain Bogardus had done. She wanted to show she could compete with the big guns, and she proved a worthy contender by coming very close. After nine hours, she had broken 4,772 balls.

On the last weekend in April, Oakley and Butler showed up at Louisville Baseball Park, where the Wild West show had pitched camp. They looked around but could not find Cody. Oakley decided to get some practice before the show began that afternoon. She and Butler carried their shotguns into the arena. Oakley noticed a man standing at the corner of the grandstand. He wore a knee-length coat and a derby hat and carried a fancy cane. Dressed like a city slicker, he certainly did not look like he belonged with the Wild West. Thinking he was just a random spectator, Oakley paid little attention to him. She picked up a shotgun and began to practice. Butler winged clay pigeons from a trap, and Oakley shot them to rubble. She fired quickly, with her gun upside down or right-side up, in her left hand or her right. When she finished, she lowered her smoking gun.

Suddenly, the stranger came running toward her. "Fine! Wonderful!" he shouted, as quoted in *Annie Oakley*. "Have you got some photographs with your gun?" Much to Oakley's surprise, this odd-looking man was Nate Salsbury, the business manager of the Wild West show. He was so impressed with Oakley's performance that he hired her on the spot, without even consulting Cody first. According to Salsbury, a woman sharpshooter in the lineup would draw quite a crowd, especially a woman who could shoot as she did.

Although Oakley was practically unknown, she immediately secured a solo spot in the program. Butler humbly stepped aside to let his talented wife take center stage. She appeared midway through the program, after the riding of the Pony Express and Buffalo Bill's staged duel with Cheyenne chief Yellow Hand. In time, though, she was promoted to the No. 2 spot. Her act was short, lasting only about 10 minutes, but it brimmed with charm and jaw-dropping stunts. Audiences fell in love with her just seconds into her act. She skipped in from the grandstand gangway, waving and blowing kisses, wearing a short skirt, usually blue or light brown, that fell just below her knees. She embroidered flowers on her skirts and stitched ribbon trim along the hems. Her blouse hung loosely around her waist, allowing her the freedom of movement she needed to shoot. Yet, her collar was stiffly starched, giving her a wholesome, refined look. As an added touch, she pinned a six-pointed star to her sombrero and laced up a pair of pearl-buttoned leggings.

Annie Oakley was such a sure shot that she could aim and shoot a small glass ball that was whirled on the end of a string while using a hand mirror and with her back turned. In this picture Oakley is performing the stunt.

With her wide array of amazing shots, Oakley quickly became a star performer. She shattered balls while firing a rifle held upside down over her head or while she was lying on her back. Sometimes, Butler would take a rope with balls attached to the end of it and twirl it over his head while Oakley blew them to shards, one by one. She did more than just stun audiences with her dead-on shooting, however. Oakley also wowed spectators with her athletic skills. Quick and agile, she would grab a glass ball and throw it up herself. The ball sailed high and long, surprising anyone who thought women could not throw. Then, she would grab her gun, fire, and hit the ball in midair. At times, she tossed up two balls at one time. She shot one right away, and then she twirled completely around and smashed the other one before it hit the ground. Although she seldom bragged about her skill, Oakley always spoke matter-of-factly about it. "I feel now and then," she once said, as quoted in *Annie Oakley*, "as if I could not miss."

Audiences especially liked her mirror shot. In this stunt, Oakley turned her back to the target and aimed by sighting it in a hand-held mirror or, sometimes, even a shiny table knife. In another feat, totally of her own creation and equally as popular, she laid a shotgun in the dirt about 10 feet on the far side of her gun table. Then, she hurried back to her mark on the other side. As soon as Butler released a clay bird from the trap, she ran toward her gun, hurdling the table. She picked up her gun and shot the bird before it hit the dirt. The stunt was quite impressive, considering she only had five seconds to do it.

To understand just how fast Oakley was with her gun, a newspaper once timed her during a stunt. In this performance, Butler stood on a chair and held out a 4-inch (10-cm) tin disk. Oakley stood with her back to him, and called out, "Pull!" Butler dropped the disk. Oakley spun around, fired, and pinged it before it hit the floor. According to the newspaper, a falling object drops 16 feet (4.8 m) in a second. Because Butler held the disk 8 feet (2.4 m) off the floor, Oakley had to turn and sight it in just half a second.

After her 10 minutes on stage were over, she skipped across the arena and disappeared behind the curtains. Just before she ducked out of sight, she lifted her leg in a little kick. That playful kick became a signature closing to Oakley's act. It was as much a mark of her showmanship as was the silver star on her hat. Oakley quickly put Buffalo Bill's worries to ease. She had no trouble filling the spot of Captain Bogardus. In fact, Nate Salsbury boldly said she "laid the captain away in the shade."

REUNITED WITH SITTING BULL

Wild West advertising agent John Burke stepped off a train at the Atlantic Express depot in Buffalo, New York. "He is ours. I have captured him," he announced to reporters, as quoted in *The Life and Legacy of Annie Oakley*. Lakota Sioux chief Sitting Bull emerged from the train and joined Burke on the depot platform. The Lakota chief wore a beaded, buckskin tunic and an elaborate headdress decorated with eagle feathers. In one hand, he grasped a bow and arrows. In the other, he held a long peace pipe. He followed Burke into an open carriage, and they rode down Michigan Street toward the park where the Wild West was performing.

In reality, Sitting Bull was not a prisoner of Burke's. But Burke had fought so hard to get him to New York, it almost seemed as if he had won a bitter battle. He had gone all the way to the Standing Rock Reservation in South Dakota, where Sitting Bull lived. There, he tried to persuade Sitting Bull to travel with the show for one season. According to legend, Sitting Bull refused Burke's pleas time and time again, until someone showed him a picture of Annie Oakley—the young lady he had adopted as Little Sure Shot. At once, Sitting Bull's eyes lit up. Seeing this reaction as an opportunity, Burke told Sitting Bull that, if he joined the Wild West, he could see Oakley every day. Whether or not the story is true, Sitting Bull at last agreed to spend 1885 on tour with Wild West.

That year, Little Sure Shot was somewhat overshadowed by the famous Lakota chief. Oakley, however, did not mind sharing the spotlight. She and Butler had finally found a steady income with the Wild West. For the most part, Oakley's first season was a total success. The only hardship she experienced was when Butler's poodle,

George, caught pneumonia and died. A carpenter who traveled with the show built a small wooden coffin for George, and Oakley and Butler covered the dog's body with a satin and velvet tablecloth they had used in their act. After the Wild West crew said their goodbyes, Oakley and Butler buried their beloved pooch in a friend's yard in Cleveland, Ohio.

5

RIVAL SHOOTER

During the summer of 1886, the Wild West performed at Erastina, the new, open-air amphitheater on Staten Island, New York. A few new acts joined the show, including Lillian Smith, a 15-year-old shooter from Coleville, California. Bill Cody described Smith as "The Champion Rifle Shot of the World." In one of her stunts, Smith shattered 20 glass balls in 24 seconds using a Winchester rifle. As soon as she arrived at Erastina, she began to brag that "Annie Oakley was done for." She planned to take over as the new hotshot female shooter of the Wild West.

Oakley immediately recognized Smith as a rival act. Smith performed seventh in the show, just one act away from Oakley, who now shot fifth. In her act, Smith broke 25 glass balls in a minute, shattered balls that were attached to strings and spinning around a pole, and pinged a plate 35 times in 15 seconds. Smith, however, had far less class than Oakley. She constantly bragged about her skills, dressed seductively, and flirted with the Wild West cowboys. To feel less threatened by Smith's youthful edge, Oakley knocked six years off her age. She began to tell people she was born in 1866 instead of 1860. Because of her tiny frame and childlike face, it was not hard for Oakley to convince people she was 20 years old. Oakley's lie became so widely accepted that her actual date of birth was left off her gravestone.

Still, Oakley wanted to outshine her competitor. At the opening parade in New York City, she set out to capture the attention of

Above is a publicity photo used to advertise Annie Oakley and Buffalo Bill's Wild West show. Although she appeared girlish and demure, Oakley could take on any man or woman when it came to sharpshooting.

spectators. She created a new outfit, with the name "Oakley" stitched on the front and the back. Her plan backfired horribly, however. Days before the parade, Oakley had come down with a serious ear infection. Instead of traveling the 7-mile (11-km) parade route, she should have been resting in bed. At the end of the parade, she had to be lifted off her horse and carried to her tent. Her ear bled for nearly five hours. The next morning, a doctor diagnosed Oakley with blood poisoning. Because of the severe infection, she lost four days of work, while Smith took her place on stage. Years later, Oakley wrote that those four days were the only ones during her 40-year career in which she missed a show.

Before long, Oakley was back on stage and once again drawing crowds. During the first month, the Wild West was attracting 14,000 spectators a day. Many days, the show completely sold out. The show's carpenters decided to build more grandstands to accommodate the swelling crowds. During the winter of 1886–1887, the Wild West performed a new four-act show called the "Dawn of Civilization" at Madison Square Garden in New York City. In the show, Oakley did her usual shooting routine, but she also debuted a new riding stunt. While dangling from a sidesaddle, she untied a handkerchief that had been knotted just above one of the horse's hooves. In another trick, she tossed her hat on the ground and then charged toward it on horseback. As she rode past the hat, she reached down and snatched it up. Amazed by her superior riding skills, the New York Ladies Riding Club awarded Oakley a special gold medal.

Throughout the 1886 season, tensions began to build between Oakley and Buffalo Bill. Perhaps Oakley was annoyed by Cody's decision to hire Lillian Smith. She may have seen his actions as a lack of confidence in her abilities. The relationship continued to sour as the 1887 season approached. To get her mind off the discord, Oakley returned to Ohio early that spring to visit family and friends. Meanwhile, Frank Butler prepared for the season ahead, which would take them overseas to England.

A YEAR IN LONDON

In April 1887, the Wild West sailed to London, England, to help celebrate the fiftieth anniversary of Queen Victoria's coronation. The event was called Queen Victoria's Golden Jubilee. Undoubtedly, the scene on the Hudson River that day resembled the loading of Noah's Ark. Crowds gathered around the docks to watch as 180 horses, 18 buffalo, and numbers of elk, mules, steers, and donkeys made their way up the gangplank to the steamship *State of Nebraska*.

In London, the Wild West set up camp at Earl's Court, which consisted of 23 acres (9 hectares) of gardens, courtyards, and exhibition halls. Horse stables, a corral, and a 20,000-seat grandstand had all been built just for the occasion. Finally, Oakley and Butler enjoyed some luxurious living quarters. Each tent had a wooden floor and a stove for heating. The show opened on May 9 to a full house, and the crowds kept coming. During the first three weeks, the Wild West attracted 500,000 spectators. Much to Oakley's delight, she captured most of the attention given to the female shooters. At last, she could feel confident that Smith was no real threat to her.

The Wild West was so popular in England that high-profile government officials hosted certain performances. Former Prime Minister William Gladstone served as host, as did Edward, Prince of Wales—Queen Victoria's oldest son who would one day become King Edward VII. Prince Edward was known as a lady's man and a terrible flirt. Princess Alexandra, who had been married to Edward for 24 years, knew about his indiscretions but did nothing to end them. She was a quiet woman who suffered from a serious illness and thought it best just to ignore the situation. Oakley had heard the rumors and had compassion for Alexandra.

During one show, Prince Edward and his family took their seats in the royal box. After Oakley's performance, Edward called her up to the royal box to congratulate her on her shooting. He extended his arm to her for a handshake. Instead of taking his hand, Oakley turned to Princess Alexandra and shook her hand first. "You'll have to excuse me, please," Oakley said to Edward, as recorded in *Annie Oakley*, "because I am an American and in America, ladies come first." Some newspapers scolded Oakley for her behavior. In English custom, it was rude to snub the prince and turn to his wife first. But Oakley was proud of her actions. She believed the incident gave Princess Alexandra some much-needed revenge over her husband's flirtatious escapades. Lillian Smith, however, was not nearly as bold

In 1887, the British Empire celebrated Queen Victoria's fiftieth anniversary of her accession (*shown above*). In England, Buffalo Bill's Wild West show received a tremendous reception, with two and a half million people coming to see the performance and several other shows. Annie Oakley, who performed for the queen and other crowned heads of state, was lavished with praise and newspapers declared her "far and away" the show's best.

as Oakley. Another night, the prince called Smith up to the royal box, and she had no problem accepting his handshake.

In England, Oakley was a favorite with audiences. Almost every day, she received invitations to tea parties and luncheons with members of high society. Her tent was always full of flowers, sent to her by fans. One newspaper noted, "The loudest applause of the night is reserved for Miss Annie Oakley." While in Europe, Oakley received four marriage proposals. One offer was from a French count, who threatened to kill himself if Oakley did not accept. Because Oakley and Butler did not have the same last name, many people thought she was single. But Oakley was not the least bit tempted by the count. He had sent her his picture along with his proposal. Oakley shot a bullet through his head in the photograph, wrote "respectfully declined" on the back, and mailed it to the count. Oakley also received gifts from her admirers. That summer, she was given a carriage, a clock, a silk dress, a thoroughbred English horse, and a St. Bernard puppy. Butler did not seem to mind all the attention his wife attracted. The more the crowds applauded her, the happier he seemed to be.

Every summer, the best shooters in England gathered on the Wimbledon Commons recreation ground in London for a rifle-shooting event. In 1887, everyone in England expected the big-name shooters from the Wild West—Buffalo Bill Cody, Lillian Smith, and Annie Oakley—to show up. On July 19, Smith was the first to drop by the event. During her tour of the grounds, she stopped at the running deer target—an iron target in the shape of a deer that a shooter had to hit while it was moving. She picked up a rifle and stepped up to the mark. Her shooting attempt was a disaster. The first two bullets completely missed the target, and the next shots hit the haunch, or the upper leg, of the iron deer. At seeing the shots, some spectators started to chuckle. Hitting the haunch was considered worse than missing the target. If it had been a real deer, the shot would not have killed the deer, but it would have escaped only to suffer. Moreover, at Wimbledon, anyone who hit the haunch had to pay a fine. Embarrassed, Smith claimed that she had missed the target because the rifle she used was heavier than her own. She promised to come back with her own rifle and try again. Smith, however, never returned.

The next day, Oakley appeared at Wimbledon. Although she was not a rifle shooter, which was supposed to be Smith's area of expertise, she tried her hand at the running deer target. Oakley did a much better job at hitting the target than her rival had done. Her success was a huge blow to Smith. Oakley, a shotgun expert, had beaten Smith at her own game. Things continued to worsen for Smith when a skeptical spectator accused her of cheating. In one of her acts, Smith claimed to hit a ball that was spinning

Mastering the Blue Rocks

During the summer of 1887, Annie Oakley made her first attempt at shooting English clay pigeons, called "blue rocks." These birds were smaller and much faster than American pigeons. "They go like lightning," Frank Butler said of the blue rocks, as quoted in *Annie Oakley* by Shirl Kasper. Blue rocks were so hard to shoot, Oakley hit only five birds out of 20 on her first try. Oakley might have never mastered the blue rocks if it had not been for Charles Lancaster, an English gunmaker.

Lancaster noticed that the gun Oakley was using to shoot at the blue rocks was not the right fit for her. In his opinion, the gun was too heavy at 7.5 pounds (3.4 kg). Because of the weight, the gun dropped when Oakley fired it, causing her to shoot under the birds. He offered to design a lighter gun for her. Lancaster made a 12-gauge, 28-inch (71-cm) double-barreled shotgun with a short stock and an easy trigger pull. It weighed just six pounds (2.7 kg), much lighter than her old gun. When Oakley tried it out on the blue rocks, she was right on the mark.

One day in June, Oakley gave a private shooting exhibition at the prestigious London Gun Club at Notting Hill. To prove her worth as a true sportsman, she needed to do well in this performance. At the show, Oakley performed most of her regular feats, but she added one more to the list. She planned to shoot at 25 lightning-fast blue rocks. Oakley's Lancaster gun did not let her down. She nailed 18 of the birds. After the exhibition, Lord Stormont, the president of the gun club, awarded Oakley a special gold medal. A drawing of the Notting Hill grounds was engraved on the medal, as well as the words "Presented to Miss Annie Oakley by the members of the London Gun Club, June 11, 1887." This medal was the first ever awarded by the club. It would be Oakley's all-time favorite achievement, and she wore it for her publicity photos. Later, Oakley added another inscription on the back side of the medal. The words were those spoken by Prince Edward about her achievement: "I know of no one more worthy of it."

3,000 times per minute. A test of the speed revealed that the ball spun only 362 times. With Smith exposed as a fraud, Oakley no longer had to worry about a competitor. In fact, she even started to get more credit than the show's owner.

When Buffalo Bill failed to show up at Wimbledon, Oakley's fine shooting made a mockery of him. At least Smith had been brave enough to try. Sportsmen wondered why Cody, who was now known also as "The Colonel," would not take a crack at the running deer. Perhaps, they assumed, he was afraid he would miss. And so, newspaper reporters hailed Oakley as the real champion of the Wild West. When Oakley started to steal the show away from Buffalo Bill, their relationship became more strained. In addition, Oakley had been doing some work outside of the Wild West. She was giving shooting lessons and took exhibition jobs at gun clubs. Oakley was making some good money on the side, and this knowledge undoubtedly irritated Cody. With tensions continuing to boil, Oakley and Butler made a daring move. They decided to quit the Wild West and start their own show, featuring Little Sure Shot Annie Oakley.

6

A NEW SHOW

In December 1887, Frank Butler and Annie Oakley returned to New York City from London alone, while Buffalo Bill's Wild West stayed in England until the following May. They moved into a small apartment overlooking Madison Square Garden. Then Butler went to work putting together a new show called Little Sure Shot, the Pony Express.

Meanwhile, Butler managed to bring in a little money by setting up shooting matches and exhibition shows for Oakley. Her first match took place on January 16, 1888, in Merchantville, New Jersey. She prepared to challenge Englishman William Graham, who was touring the United States and beating all the best American shooters. The temperature hovered around zero (-18° Celsius), as a sharp breeze and a steady sleet cut through the air. Butler rubbed brandy over Oakley's hands and arms to keep her warm. As the match began, Oakley pulled out the Lancaster she had used to shoot down blue rock pigeons in London. On this day, however, she lost the match, shooting down 33 clay pigeons to Graham's 36.

Two weeks later, she faced Graham again, this time in Easton, Pennsylvania. When she got to town, she checked into Room 13 of a hotel in Easton. Her superstitious fans begged her to switch rooms, believing the number 13 would jinx her match. Oakley refused to listen to them. Her skill proved stronger than superstition. She beat

Graham 24 to 19. On February 22, she met Graham for a third deciding match. Once again, she stayed in Room 13, just to spite the skeptics. She won the match 47 to 45.

Oakley competed in a number of other money matches. She defeated famed shooter Phil Daly Jr. and New Jersey state champion Miles Johnson. She did not win every match, though. On at least two occasions, she lost, once to Al Bandle, an old friend from Cincinnati, Ohio, and another match against Phil Daly. Between matches, she performed exhibition shows. In one show, she broke 100 out of 109 glass balls in 3 minutes and 10 seconds. She also set an American record in doubles shooting, hitting 25 pairs of balls in a row.

Even with all of the competitions and exhibitions, Butler and Oakley struggled to make ends meet. They decided to pick up extra cash doing acts at the variety theaters. Oakley joined the show of singer-songwriter Tony Pastor. She performed at the Criterion in Brooklyn, New York; the Howard Atheneum in Boston, Massachusetts; and Jacob and Proctor's in Hartford, Connecticut.

In the spring of 1888, Butler learned that another American Wild West show was struggling. Pawnee Bill's Historical Wild West Exhibition and Indian Encampment was nearly broke and needed a big act to save it. Pawnee Bill's real name was Gordon W. Lillie, and he had at one time traveled with Buffalo Bill's Wild West. Butler had an idea to get Oakley a headlining act in a Wild West show. He talked the owner of Comanche Bill's Wild West into buying Pawnee Bill's show and combining the two shows. However, the new show wasn't as popular as Butler had hoped. After just one month, Oakley quit Pawnee Bill's show and rejoined Tony Pastor on his fall tour. It turned out to be a good choice. By late October, Pawnee Bill's show was again broke and split up.

By the end of fall, Butler had finally found someone to finance the western show he had wanted for Oakley when they left Buffalo Bill's Wild West. He renamed his Little Sure Shot show *Deadwood Dick: Or the Sunbeam of the Sierras*. In the drama, Oakley played Sunbeam, a white girl who had been taken prisoner when a group of

Although Pawnee Bill advertised Annie Oakley heavily and made the most of her talent—despite having a wife who was also a sharpshooter with the show—Pawnee Bill's Wild West show was unsuccessful. Oakley left the show after a month.

American Indians attacked her family's covered wagon. She grew up as part of the American Indian village, learning how to shoot a gun with amazing accuracy. A typical western melodrama of the age, the show offered many thrilling scenes. In fact, 25 characters were shot dead during its three acts. The show opened on Christmas Eve 1888 at the New Standard Theatre in Philadelphia, Pennsylvania. The play, however, turned out to be a flop and suffered brutal reviews. Oakley's early career as an actress lasted only one month. In January 1889, the show closed.

IN EUROPE

At some point during the summer of 1888, Oakley and Buffalo Bill reconciled their differences. She rejoined the Wild West and set sail for Paris, France, in April 1889. The Wild West's first stop was that year's world's fair—the Paris Universal Exposition of 1889—in celebration of the one-hundredth anniversary of the French Revolution. Luckily for Buffalo Bill, Oakley was back with the show. If she hadn't been part of the performance, the Wild West might have failed.

A mountainous cultural barrier stood between the French and the Americans, much greater than any cast member of the Wild West could have imagined. Unfamiliar with U.S. history or American Indian groups, the Parisian audience did not understand what *Wild West* even meant. They sat confused, barely applauding the opening acts. Just as the show was heading for disaster, Oakley took the stage. As she peered out across the crowd, she noticed how stiff and serious they were. "They sat like icebergs at first," she later wrote. The only people ready to applaud were the show's paid "clackers"—people who sat on the fringes of the stands and signaled the audience to clap at the right moment. Butler, however, silenced the clackers. "I wanted honest applause or none at all," Oakley said.

When Oakley's first shot shattered the target, the crowd's eyes widened. They did not need to speak English to know a good shot when they saw one. As Oakley fired faster and faster, the audience responded with "oohs," "ahs," and "bravos." At the end of her act, the crowd roared and tossed handkerchiefs into the air. Oakley had saved the show.

Oakley's opening night might have had a much different ending, though. She had brought along 50 pounds (23 kg) of her favorite English Schultze gunpowder. But when the Wild West docked in France, she learned that she could not bring it off the ship. France had a monopoly on gunpowder, and the use of English gunpowder was illegal. Oakley did not have time to experiment with a new brand. She needed the Schultze powder to shoot well. "It not only meant success for myself," she said, as quoted in *Annie Oakley*, "but for the Wild West company." She only had one choice—to smuggle in her powder.

Oakley grabbed five hot-water bottles and poured the Schultze powder into each of them. Then, she found four other women to be her partners in crime. Each woman put on a dress with a bustle. They hid the water bottle of powder in the poofy fabric of the bustle. It was the first time Oakley had ever worn a dress with a bustle, but she was glad to do it. That smuggled powder made all the difference.

While performing in Paris, Oakley met President Sadi Carnot of France. He was so impressed with her shooting skills that he thought she would make a fine soldier. "When you feel like changing your nationality and profession," he told her, "there is a commission awaiting you in the French Army." The West African king of Senegal had similar thoughts. He wanted Oakley to come to his country to shoot wild tigers.

In Paris, Oakley added a new stunt to her act. She noticed that the Frenchmen were poor rifle shots, but handy with pistols. She watched pistol shooter Ira Paine put a bullet through a playing card. Oakley decided to create her own version of the trick. She fired a pistol at the ace of hearts. After shooting it head on, she turned the card sideways and split it down the edge with a bullet. This pistol stunt became one of her best-known acts.

While at the exposition, Oakley met the famous inventor Thomas Edison, who was most noted for his invention of the light bulb. Edison's phonograph was one of the star attractions at the exposition. After struggling to get used to French gunpowder, Oakley decided to ask Edison a strange question. She wondered if he had ever considered inventing an electric gun. Edison admitted he had not thought of that possibility, but maybe one day he would create one. Although he never invented an electric gun, Edison found other ways to help the Wild West. Several years later, he designed an electrical set that allowed the Wild West to perform at night.

Edison also made Oakley into one of the world's first movie stars. In the fall of 1894, he invited her to his studio in West Orange, New Jersey, to test his newest invention—a kinetograph, an early version of the movie camera. Edison wanted to see whether his invention could capture Oakley's gun smoke on film. Much to his delight, the kinetograph not only recorded the gun smoke but also the shards of glass from Oakley's exploding balls. Later, Edison's first short films debuted in nickelodeons—early movie theaters that charged a five-cent admission. Oakley's brief gun-slinging clip was probably one of the movies played.

In the fall of 1889, the Universal Exposition closed. The Wild West left Paris and embarked on a three-year tour of Europe. Oakley continued to impress shooters at local gun clubs and to charm world leaders. During one performance, Crown Prince Wilhelm of Germany watched Oakley shoot the tip off a cigarette that Butler held in his mouth. Perhaps thinking the stunt was just a trick, he asked Oakley to repeat the stunt, this time while he held the cigarette. Not wanting to risk harming the crown prince, Oakley agreed to do the stunt only if he held the cigarette in a long holder instead of just between his lips. As it turned out, she had nothing to worry about. As always, her aim was true, and she shot the ashes clean off. Crown Prince Wilhelm would later be blamed for starting World War I (1914–1918). Years later, people often teased Oakley that she had missed her chance to prevent the war—if only she had hit Wilhelm instead of the cigarette.

The Wild West tour took Oakley all over Europe, including Italy, Germany, Austria, Spain, and Great Britain. In their spare time, she and Butler did as much sightseeing as they could. In Italy, they climbed to the top of Mount Vesuvius and visited the buried city of Pompeii. They also took a gondola ride down the Grand Canal in Venice. Over Christmas, Oakley and Butler spent some time in Kent, England. There, Oakley picked up a newspaper and read some startling news. According to one article, she had died of a lung disease in Buenos Aires, Argentina. Soon, the crazy story was being published in newspapers all over Europe and America. When Oakley's mother read the news in a Cincinnati paper, she cried for two days until she finally learned it was not true.

In April 1891, Oakley went on a second tour of Europe with the Wild West. Now 31, the first delicate lines of wrinkles appeared on her face—a result of constant exposure to outdoor weather. But her aim was as straight as it ever had been. On October 27, 1892, she and Butler finally arrived home in New York. By this time, the name Annie Oakley was known in every corner of Europe and America.

MAKING A HOME IN NUTLEY

After they returned from Europe, Butler and Oakley started to look for a home in northern New Jersey. They bought a lot in Nutley, a pretty little town on the Passaic River, just 13 miles (21 km) from New York City. There, they began to build their dream home. Buffalo Bill was planning to open another long-running show in South Brooklyn. Rumors even circled that he might stay there permanently. After years of touring, Oakley looked forward to settling down and making a home in Nutley.

Oakley and Butler moved into their new house at 304 Grant Avenue in December 1893. It was a large, three-story house, with a front porch and a railed balcony on an upper level. Oakley also set aside a "sportsmen's room" in her new home and asked hunters to contribute mounted birds and animal heads or skins to her collection. She promised to give proper credit to each donation by labeling it with the hunter's name. Wanting to give Oakley a special house-warming gift, one fan asked the sportsmen of America to give a dollar each toward a present. He raised enough donations to present Oakley with a solid silver tea set. Although Oakley was a simple person, the silver did not look out of place in her home. She enjoyed being a lady and decorating her house with fine objects. She

Annie Oakley was one of the best trick shooters around. From 30 paces, she could shoot a playing card on its edge in half, hit a dime thrown into the air, cut a cigarette hanging from her husband's lips, or break glass balls while standing on the back of a galloping horse.

had a vast collection of crystal and furnished the rooms with beautiful fabrics and lovely embroidery. Of course, Oakley did the sewing herself.

In March 1894, Oakley and Butler were invited to participate in the Nutley Amateur Circus. The money raised in this charity event went to the Red Cross. Before Oakley performed, a reporter found her practicing behind Eaton Stone's barn, where the circus was being held. The reporter asked her what kind of skills someone needed to become a dead shot, like herself. "I suppose it's a gift, though practice helps," Oakley answered, as quoted in *Annie Oakley*. "Still,

Cheaters

In fancy shooting, cheaters were common. One of Oakley's favorite stunts was shooting the ashes off a cigarette. This feat was quite easy for others to fake. The shooter's assistant simply attached a wire to the cigarette. As soon as the gun fired, the assistant would touch the wire with his tongue. The vibration made the ashes fall off the cigarette. Oakley's candle trick could also be done by cheaters. Instead of placing the candle out in the open, the shooter could set it in front of a block of wood. If the bullet passed anywhere near the candle, the wind movement—caught by the wood block—would snuff the flame out.

Oakley made her stunts look so easy she was often accused of cheating. On one occasion, a man in the crowd was convinced that her feats were trickery. He offered her his watch and told her to throw it up and shoot it. Oakley did just as the man requested, smashing the watch to pieces. "He has never been able to tell the time by that watch since," Oakley later joked in *Annie Oakley* by Shirl Kasper.

I've gone months without touching a gun, and then stepped into the ring without preliminary practice and made as good a score as I ever did." She went on to explain. "It's a matter of feeling," she said. "The marksman who hesitates is lost. Just take it for granted you are going to hit and fire away before you have time to doubt the certainty of success."

That night, Oakley performed a stunt she had never before done in public. She stood up on the back of her horse, and as the horse circled the arena, she shattered glass balls, one after another. It was the biggest act of the entire evening.

On May 12, 1894, the Wild West opened its new season at Ambrose Park in South Brooklyn. Before the show set up, the park had been an old cinder dump. Now, it held the largest arena the Wild West had ever built, measuring 450 feet (137 m) long by 312 feet

(95 m) wide, with a towering backdrop of the Bighorn Mountains. The Wild West's new grand entrance act was even more thrilling than it had been years ago at Erastina. The show had added troops of soldiers from all over the world, offering a kaleidoscope of colors. A new electric light system also allowed for performances at night.

Even with all the improvements, the season was not as successful as Buffalo Bill had hoped. When the show closed on October 6, Cody put aside any plans for setting up a permanent arena in South Brooklyn. Instead, he struck a deal with a circus owner named James A. Bailey, one of the creators of the Barnum & Bailey's Circus. The Wild West would go on the road again, this time on a U.S. tour.

7

ON THE ROAD

William Cody's circus deal put James Bailey in charge of the three largest touring shows—Buffalo Bill's Wild West, the Barnum & Bailey Circus, and the Ringling Brothers Circus. The tour would be rigorous. Annie Oakley would be performing one-night shows in hundreds of towns and cities across the United States. In 1895, the Wild West made 131 stops along the railroad lines. The following year, the show played in 132 towns. While many of the show's workers had to suffer with cramped quarters, Oakley and Frank Butler had much more comfortable accommodations. They had a full bedroom, complete with a dresser and two plush chairs. They even had running water in their room. To make the place feel more like home, Oakley sewed a pretty bedspread and matching curtains to hang in the train car windows.

The Wild West had only a short time to set up an enormous campsite. As soon as the train stopped, the hired hands went to work. They pounded in stakes and roped up the canvas grandstand tent, which was stitched together out of 22,750 yards (20,802 m) of canvas. One newspaper described the tent as being so big "a person sitting on one end of it would need a spyglass [binoculars] . . . to [see] a friend at the other end." The crew also set up numerous tent shops for the cast, including a barber shop, repair shop, blacksmith shop, and a laundry tent. The Wild West was like a little village, completely self-sufficient. Even the glass balls Oakley shot in her act were molded at the camp.

Life on the road meant constantly being on the move. The train rolled into the station at dawn, and the crew set up the lot. As soon as the arena was up, the cast marched a parade through town. The show performed at 2:00 P.M. and again at 8:00 that night. Then the crew tore down the tents, packed up the show, and the train cars rolled out of town. The whole routine started again at sunup the next day. By 1898, Oakley had fired her guns in towns all across the country. She performed her act two times a day, six days a week. People often asked her how many shells she fired in her lifetime. In one year she used 40,000 shot shells and several thousand ball cartridges. Yet, she rarely got tired of shooting. "While shooting, I scarce realize that I have a gun in my hands," she told one reporter, as quoted in *Annie Oakley* by Shirl Kasper.

By 1900, Americans from every corner of the country had seen Buffalo Bill's Wild West, featuring Little Sure Shot. The name Annie Oakley appeared in thousands of advertisements and newspaper articles. She was a legend of the American West. Still, it was hard work, and Oakley sometimes considered retiring from the show. In 1899, she said, "I have thought several times I would not go with the show another year, but I always do."

After a long season on the road, Oakley and Butler often vacationed in the South. They hunted game in the Blue Ridge Mountains of Virginia, near Hot Springs, Arkansas, and in the woodlands of Crowson, Tennessee, where Davy Crockett once hunted. In Hot Springs, they went hunting with John J. Sumpter Jr. and his wife. Sumpter was a skilled, local hunter, but he had a hard time keeping up with Oakley's lightning-fast shots. "Why, she kills quail while you are getting your gun to the shoulder," he said, as quoted in *Annie Oakley*. "Twice I shot her bird after she had killed it—couldn't get there quick enough."

Besides hunting vacations, Oakley and Butler also visited Darke County whenever they had time off. Oakley's mother, Susan, still lived on the family farm, and her sisters Hulda and Emily lived nearby. During these off-season visits, Oakley got to know her nieces and nephews. She was especially fond of Hulda's daughter, Fern, who later wrote a biography of Oakley titled *Missie*. Little Fern watched Oakley sew new costumes or mend her old ones. Oakley brushed them, sponged them with soapy water, and pressed them. Then, she wrapped them in tissue paper to keep them from wrinkling and packed them in her traveling trunk.

Fern idolized her famous aunt and wanted to be just like her. After watching Oakley sew, Fern decided to make her own doll dresses. One day, she accidentally cut into some fabric that her mother was using to sew a dress for Oakley. Having bought just enough fabric to make the dress, Fern's mistake meant that the dress could not be completed. Hulda was upset and wanted to punish her daughter for ruining the dress. Aunt Annie came to the rescue, though. She told Hulda that she could use the fabric to make a dress for Fern instead. Then, she told Fern that one day she could sew her aunt a dress to make up for the one she had ruined. Fern agreed, and when she grew up, she sewed Oakley several dresses.

Oakley performed in Darke County for the first time in July 1900. The Wild West set up camp in Greenville, where little Annie Moses had sold bunches of quail at the Katzenberger store. Oakley performed her act with perfection, just as always, before a crowd of 10,000 people, including her mother and sisters. In the middle of her act, two representatives of Greenville interrupted her. They presented her with a silver trophy cup, with a golden inscription reading: "To Miss Annie Oakley, From Old Friends in Greenville, O., July 25, 1900." Oakley was overcome with deep emotion. Tears streamed down her cheeks as she said, "Thank you, and God bless you all."

For the rest of her life, Oakley treasured the silver cup more than any other medal or trophy she received. Over her career, she accumulated 27 gold medals, as well as numerous rings, bracelets, pins, necklaces, and other gifts. But the silver trophy cup from Darke County meant so much to her that she had the trophy featured on her Wild West poster—right in the top center spot.

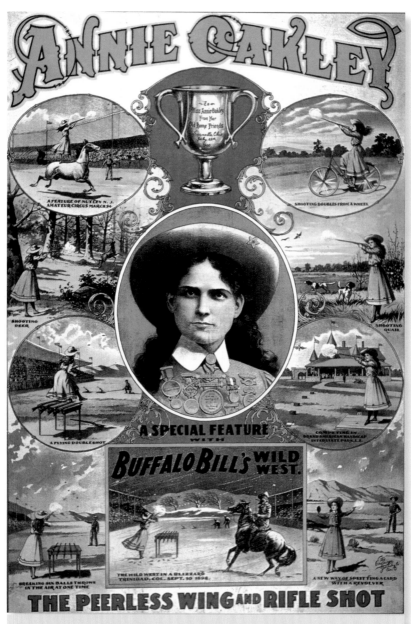

On July 25, 1900, Annie Oakley returned to her hometown of Greenville, Ohio, to perform with the Wild West show. During her visit she was given a commemorative silver cup by the townspeople. Oakley was so proud of the cup that she featured it in posters for the show.

WESTERN GIRL AND A FRAUD

The Wild West's 1901 season dragged out as usual, and Oakley and Butler were looking forward to the off-season break. The last show dates were scheduled for October 28, in Charlotte, North Carolina, and October 29, in Danville, Virginia. On October 28, Oakley finished her act, blew a kiss to the crowd, and skipped out of the arena with her signature little kick, the same as she had done for 17 years. No one could have imagined that this performance would be Annie Oakley's last act with Buffalo Bill's Wild West—not even Oakley.

All through the night, the train rumbled down the tracks toward Danville. Around 3:00 in the morning, the headlights of another train suddenly appeared out of the darkness. It was heading straight for the Wild West train. There was no time to stop. Moments later, the two trains collided head-on. Five of the show's horse cars went tumbling into the ditch. Not a single horse in any of the five cars survived. Only four people were injured, however, and no one died in the crash. Fortunately, all the cast of the Wild West was safe. Still, the final show of the season was canceled, and Oakley and Butler took their annual vacation to Hot Springs, Arkansas.

In late December, Oakley visited the baths of a Hot Springs health resort. She climbed into a scalding hot bath, which was supposed to be used for a 60-second treatment. The attendant forgot about her, however, and left her in the bath waters for 40 minutes. According to a newspaper clipping, when Oakley's limp body was pulled out of the water, her chocolate brown hair had turned completely white, all the way to the roots. Her face and hands were speckled with liver-colored spots, and she had numerous blisters on her back. For more than an hour, Oakley lay unconscious. At last, she revived, but her life would never be the same.

Oakley's Wild West image vanished into the hot springs that day. Her act hinged on her youthful appearance. How could a woman with powdered-sugar hair skip into the arena like a child? Often, Oakley liked to flip her long, dark hair over her shoulder to get a clear shot. It was all part of her stage appearance. Oakley knew her career with the Wild West was over, so she decided to quit the show.

A year later, Oakley embarked on a new career as an actress. She had become so famous that playwright Langdon McCormick wrote a play especially for her called *The Western Girl*. The story was set in Fiddletown, Colorado. Oakley played Nancy Barry, the prim and proper daughter of an outlaw bandit. Her sister was blind, and the man she loved was Lieutenant Robert Hawley, a U.S. cavalryman. Nancy's mission was to rescue anyone in trouble, including her sister and the lieutenant. For costuming, Oakley wore her Wild West garb—skirts, leggings, and sombrero. She also wore a curly, brown wig to cover her white hair. In the play, she shot a bottle out of her drunken father's hand and smashed 20 glass balls to shards. The play was a sensation, and crowds adored Oakley's performance.

The Western Girl opened in November 1902 and closed the following March. The play did so well that Oakley talked about starring in a new play by McCormick in 1903. But any future acting plans came to an end on August 11, 1903. Two days before Oakley's forty-third birthday, a scandalous newspaper story appeared in the Chicago *Examiner* that would change the course of her life for the next five years. The headline read: "ANNIE OAKLEY ASKS COURT FOR MERCY—Famous Woman . . . Steals to Secure Cocaine." The story claimed that Oakley had been caught stealing from an African-American man to get money to buy cocaine. In truth, the woman arrested was Maude Fontenella, who had once performed in a burlesque Wild West show as "Any Oakley." The imposter had begged the judge to give her a chance to change her life.

Within days, the story was printed in newspapers all around the country. Some headlines read, "Annie Oakley, Famous Rifle Shot, Is Destitute," and "Annie Oakley in Prison, Famous Rifle Shot of Buffalo Bill's Show a Cocaine Victim." Oakley's friends who read the stories did not believe them. In fact, anyone who knew the straight-laced Little Sure Shot knew they could not be true. Friends and fans clipped the stories and mailed them to Oakley, who was at home in Nutley. The more false stories Oakley read, the angrier she became. She sent letters to each of the newspapers, demanding a retraction.

Newspaper publisher William Randolph Hearst published a false story claiming that Annie Oakley stole money to support a drug habit. Other newspapers picked up the Hearst article, and over six years, despite the time and expense, Oakley pursued 55 libel lawsuits against them. Hoping to avoid paying a court judgment, Hearst sent a detective to Darke County to collect gossip against Oakley, but the investigator found nothing.

The newspapers did run retractions and apologized for printing the false story. Both friends and sportsmen offered Oakley their total support, but Oakley could not be consoled. The incident devastated her. "That terrible piece . . . nearly killed me," she later wrote. "The only thing that kept me alive was the desire to purge my character." She refused to rest until her name was once again pure.

Determined to clear her name, Oakley launched the largest libel suit of the time. She brought 25 lawsuits demanding $25,000 each in damages against 25 newspapers that had printed the fraudulent story. Those lawsuits totaled $625,000. In the end, Oakley would sue 55 newspapers. She either won the lawsuits or settled out of court with all but one of the newspapers. For years, newspapers had always printed kind stories about Annie Oakley. But Oakley showed them no mercy. The attack on her pride and character sliced straight through to her core. Her reputation meant everything to her.

The trials began in March 1904. For the five years that followed, Oakley traveled from city to city to testify on her own behalf. She walked into the courtroom wearing a simple black dress with a red velvet collar. She wore a black veil over her face, which she lifted when she took the stand. Those in the courtroom said she reminded them of "a kindly schoolteacher," not the drug-addicted woman portrayed in the articles. One newspaper commented, "She acted the cultured lady in every respect . . . refined and almost classical."

While Oakley was appearing in court, Butler found work as a representative for the Union Metallic Cartridge Company. He traveled around the country promoting the company's products to trapshooters. In the early 1900s, states began to place restrictions on the number of animals that could be shot in a hunting season. Sportsmen still wanted to shoot after they had reached their limits and during the off-season. They took up shooting clay pigeons, a sport called trapshooting. In 1906, there were an estimated 100,000 trapshooters in America. By 1916, this number had soared to 600,000.

Because Oakley was gone to attend her trials and Butler was on the road for the Union Metallic Cartridge Company, they were rarely at home in Nutley. They decided to sell the house and moved into an apartment at 180th Street and Fort Washington Avenue in

New York City. Later, they moved to another apartment in East Orange, New Jersey.

As the trials dragged on, the stress and anxiety wore on Oakley. "There were months when I prayed to God every day to only spare my reason so as to let me clear myself of this, and I will do it," she later said. The lawsuit ordeal greatly aged her, but she vowed to push on to the end. The damages awarded were far less than she had sued for at the start. But by 1909, when the lawsuits were finally closed, the money awarded may have totaled as much as $800,000. Her legal expenses were higher than her judgments, Oakley was not so concerned about the money. She had resurrected her reputation, and she could put no price on her name.

"HAPPY EVER AFTER"

Although Annie Oakley's efforts to restore her reputation kept her busy, she still had time for other activities. She joined Frank Butler on the road, advertising for the Union Metallic Cartridge Company. Once again, she demonstrated her skills by hitting brass disks, pennies, and marbles. She even "scrambled" eggs, by bursting them with bullets from 50 yards (46 m) away. Her picture appeared on Union Metallic advertisements for sure-fire blank cartridges. In June 1907, she competed on Ladies Day at the Trenton Shooting Association Tournament, in Trenton, New Jersey. In August, she competed at the 14th Annual Target and Live Bird Tournament in Betterton, Maryland. On August 18, 1908, Oakley was visiting a gun club in Chicago, Illinois, when she received a telegram from Ohio. Her mother had died. Oakley and Butler left at once for Darke County. They buried Susan Shaw in Yorkshire Cemetery, just outside of North Star.

By 1910, the country was changing fast. The horse and wagon were becoming the transportation of the past. Railroad tracks stretched from city to city throughout the East and were snaking through the West. Automobiles dotted city streets, and the first airplanes were taking to the skies.

Yet, the memory of the Wild West had not completely faded. At 50 years old, Oakley was just as popular as she had been at 25. Audiences gathered wherever she chose to shoot, amazed at how "no object, however small" escaped her bullet. From time to time, Oakley received offers to re-enter show business. In 1910, 18 Wild West shows were touring the country. Any one of them would have jumped at the chance to have her, even with her white hair. In May, she made a guest appearance in Buffalo Bill's Wild West, which was performing at Madison Square Garden. Since she had left the show, the Wild West had merged with Pawnee Bill's show. After the performance, Bill Cody asked Oakley to rejoin the show, but she turned him down. Perhaps, she had heard rumors that Cody would soon be retiring, or maybe he did not offer her enough money.

A year later, though, she received an offer from the Young Buffalo Wild West show. This time, she accepted. The Young Buffalo show was similar to Buffalo Bill's, but the two were not connected. The show featured the holdup of a stagecoach, Pony Express riders, the pretend hanging of a horse thief, and a fight between cowboys and American Indians. Other acts included star cowboy Ambrose Means, who roped a buffalo with a lariat and singlehandedly yanked the huge beast to the ground.

Once again, Oakley was on the road. For two years, she awed crowds just as she had done in her early career. To bring back her youthful charm, she wore a brown, curly wig. She even added a new trick to her act. She twirled a lariat with her left hand and fired a gun with her right. She stayed with the Young Buffalo show until 1913, during which time the show joined with Colonel Fred Cummins Wild West and Indian Congress. On October 4, 1913, she gave her last performance as a Wild West star. At age 53, Annie Oakley retired from show business.

After retiring, Oakley and Butler built a two-story cottage on Hambrooks Bay, along the Eastern Shore of Maryland. Finally settling down for good, they adopted a black and white English setter named Dave. For some time, Oakley had wanted a good bird dog for hunting. One fall afternoon, Butler drove to East New Market. There he found Dave caged in a dirty kennel with little food. He

Pictured are Annie Oakley and Frank Butler with their beloved dog, Dave. Dave was described as the love of Oakley's and Butler's lives and was treated like one of the family.

offered to buy the dog, and the dog's owner agreed. Oakley took Dave hunting every other day, and before long, he was retrieving birds as if he had done it his entire life. Oakley and Butler, who never had children of their own, treated the dog like a member of the family.

Oakley, Butler, and Dave spent many days hunting near their home. By the end of hunting season, Oakley had killed quail, rabbits, squirrels, and ducks. When she wasn't hunting, Oakley sometimes performed exhibitions at nearby gun clubs and county fairs. In the winter months, Oakley and Butler traveled to Florida. There, she held shows to raise money for various causes. Once, in Leesburg, Florida, Oakley helped raise $150 for the Leesburg Band. The band thanked her by giving a concert in her honor. On another occasion,

Oakley heard about a pregnant woman who had been left penniless after her husband was killed in a mining accident. Perhaps the story reminded Oakley of her childhood. She probably thought about the way her poor mother had been left with nothing when Jacob Moses died. Oakley sent the woman a portion of the money she had won in a shooting competition. She wrote a letter to the local newspaper, urging others to do the same.

After all the years of traveling, most people thought that Oakley would be happy to have a home at last. But those who knew her best realized she might not be satisfied with a quiet life. "You can't cage a gypsy," Oakley once said about herself. "We had our own boat, dogs and oyster bed, and settled down to 'live happy ever after.' But I couldn't do it." Even Butler knew that the only place Oakley would truly feel at home was where she could grip a gun. "Riding, shooting, and dancing came natural to her, but she's a rotten house-keeper," he joked. They managed to find a little more excitement at a winter retreat in North Carolina. Oakley had first visited Pinehurst in January 1909. She competed at a tournament in this charming North Carolina village. Pinehurst was a haven for sportsmen of all kinds—from hunters to golfers—and Oakley immediately fell in love with the place.

In 1915, Oakley and Butler decided to take their winter vacation in Pinehurst at the Carolina Hotel. This four-story luxury hotel boasted elevators, steam heat, electric lights, and telephones in every room. In the 1910s, few hotels offered such conveniences. Some suites at the Carolina even had private baths and porches that were furnished as outdoor bedrooms. This stay was the first of many winter seasons at the Carolina Hotel. Although Oakley and Butler could certainly afford the expensive hotel, they were always frugal with their money. They helped pay their costly tab by working at the Pinehurst gun club.

For her weekly fox hunt, Oakley got out of bed at 4:00 in the morning and slipped on her tweed jacket and high boots. She headed down to the stables and saddled up her horse. She galloped down the road and through the woods to a nearby pond, where the hunt began. Besides hunting, there were many other activities to enjoy at the Carolina. There were dances on Saturday nights, and the orchestra played every Sunday evening. Each Monday morning, the women gathered in the tea room for their weekly bridge game.

Most of all, Oakley enjoyed teaching the women at Pinehurst how to use a gun. Her first lesson came about completely by accident. One Saturday, she overheard the wife of a wealthy guest talking to some other women in the Carolina ballroom about hunting. "My, how I wish I were a man so that I could shoot," the woman said. As soon as Oakley heard these words, she introduced herself to the woman. She assured the woman that being female should not prevent her from learning how to shoot. Then, she invited the woman out to the shooting range for a lesson. At the range, Oakley handed the woman a .22-caliber rifle and showed her how to hold it and how to stand properly while shooting. By the end of the day, the woman could hit a perfect bull's-eye.

After that first lesson, word spread around Pinehurst. Within months, Oakley registered her 700th student. She charged no fee for her lessons. Oakley believed that having more women enjoy the sport was payment enough. Oakley always believed that women should learn how to shoot guns. "I would like to see every woman know how to handle them as they know how to handle babies," she said, as quoted in *Annie Oakley* by Shirl Kasper. She stressed that women needed to know how to protect themselves and that a gun was the best way to do it. She encouraged women to keep a revolver in their nightstand.

About this time, the United States was entering World War I (1914–1918). On April 6, 1917, the United States declared war on Germany. Americans stood behind their country and supported the war effort. Guests at the Carolina Hotel soon found out about a new food-rationing plan ordered by the U.S. Food Administration. Mondays and Wednesdays were "wheatless" days, meaning the guests would not get any bread. On Tuesdays, no meat was served. These rations were imposed to save food to ship overseas to U.S. soldiers. No one at the hotel minded the menu cuts. They were happy to help their country.

Annie Oakley was a trailblazer and her success opened up new opportunities for women. She encouraged them to learn how to shoot for sports and protection. She is thought to have taught an estimated 15,000 women how to shoot. Pictured is Oakley (*center*) with some of her students.

Oakley was so patriotic that she made a suggestion to former President Theodore Roosevelt, who had been talking about leading a volunteer division into Europe. She offered to train a women's regiment to defend the homefront. At the time, her idea was quite radical. In those days, most people believed that women should not be soldiers. But that did not stop Oakley from trying. Roosevelt sided with popular opinion, however, and strongly opposed her idea. Oakley's proposal was not a new one to her. Years earlier, when she was touring with the Wild West, she had volunteered to join the U.S. Army during the Spanish-American War of 1898. Then, too, the army declined her offer.

Nevertheless, Oakley was determined to do something to support the war effort. She volunteered to visit army camps through the National War Work Council of the Young Men's Christian Association and War Camp Community Service. At each camp, she gave two exhibitions a day to thousands of young soldiers. As she performed one stunt after another, the cheers grew louder. One soldier told her that, if the United States had a regiment filled with shooters like Annie Oakley, they would quickly beat the German army. Oakley must have agreed. "What wouldn't I give to get a good old 'high-power' to my shoulder, station myself where the [Germans] were trying to advance and knock those square-heads down as fast as they came in view," she once said, "and believe me, I could do it." Oakley treasured those days in the army camps more than her years on the stage with Buffalo Bill, because she felt she was doing her part to serve her country.

Even Dave, Oakley's English setter, was a patriot. He became part of a fundraiser for the Red Cross. At a stand, the sign by Dave read: "Let Me Find Your Money for the Red Cross." People brought a quarter, a dollar, or whatever amount they wished to donate up to Dave. They wrapped the money in a handkerchief and let Dave smell it. Then they hid the handkerchief of money anywhere within 100 yards (91 m) of the stand. When they finished hiding the money, Dave hunted it down. People seemed to like the game. In one day, he raised $1,625.

The war ended on November 11, 1918. Two days later, Pinehurst residents held a parade. Oakley showed up for the event, armed with 10 rifles. She celebrated the U.S. victory the only way she knew how—by putting on a show.

WOMEN'S RIGHTS

Although Oakley starred in a sport that was traditionally a man's domain, she did not ally herself with the women's movement of her time. She refused to support the prevailing issue of the day: suffrage. According to *The Life and Legacy of Annie Oakley*, she regarded voting as unladylike and saw little value for women in such a reform.

Oakley never marched in suffrage parades or carried banners, and she was not a fan of the more radical activists in the women's movement. "If only the good women voted," she would say, as cited in Shirl Kasper's *Annie Oakley*. Kasper's biography quoted a reporter discussing Oakley and suffrage: "About this she does not have much to say. . . . But you get the impression that she never has been strong for equal rights as this generation understands the term." And that was true—Oakley was of a different, more conservative generation from the suffragettes of the early 1900s.

Some historians also believe that Oakley chose her political views carefully to protect her reputation. Although many women supported suffrage, many of Oakley's fans did not. She did not want to pick a side that might permanently damage her career.

Still, she did support other women's issues—particularly the right to equal wages. She had fought against prejudice to earn a living in her own career, so she recognized the constraints on women who wished or needed to work. "Rather than laboring in the political sphere for woman suffrage, Annie focused on economic rights and freedoms," Glenda Riley wrote in *The Life and Legacy of Annie Oakley*. "Year by year, as she enhanced her own economic stability and earning power, Annie became increasingly vocal and adamant about women's right to hold employment."

ACCIDENT ON DIXIE HIGHWAY

The 1920s brought an end to the golden era of the Wild West. By this time, Americans were crowding into a new kind of arena—the movie theater. At 60 years old, Oakley called herself "one of the good old has-beens." But to many others, she looked as young as ever. One reporter from the New York *Tribune* wrote, "Annie Oakley has found what Ponce de Leon sought in vain. She has come upon the spring of everlasting youth." Her hair had long ago turned white, but her eyes sparkled like a child's. During the interview, Oakley stood up and bent over, placing the palms of her hands on the floor without bending her knees. Then, she walked around the room on all fours. "Let me see any of your girls of today do that," she said.

As Oakley grew older, she became increasingly charitable. She was especially concerned about the fight to end tuberculosis. This deadly lung disease had killed two of her sisters, as well as hospitalized thousands of soldiers. She often visited tuberculosis patients in the sanatoriums near Pinehurst. Sometimes, she held an exhibition to raise money for these special hospitals. She had other ways of raising money as well. Many mornings, she woke early and picked flowers all day. Then, she made bouquets that she sold to guests at the Carolina. During the spring of 1920, Oakley made an amazing sacrifice to help those suffering from tuberculosis. She gathered up the 27 medals she had earned over the years for her shooting skill. She took them to a jeweler, had them melted down, and sold the gold. Then she donated the money to a tuberculosis sanitarium near Pinehurst.

A few years later, Oakley and Butler said goodbye to their friends at the Carolina Hotel for the last time. They planned to return to the house on Hambrooks Bay for the summer, but they would not be returning to Pinehurst the following winter. Before Oakley left town, she went to the local gun club on April 16, 1922. That day, she shattered 100 clay pigeons in a row. She shot all of them from the 16-yard (14.6-meter) line, setting a new world's record for women shooters.

Back in Maryland, Oakley continued to perform exhibitions from time to time for charity. At least for a moment, she even considered trying a career in the movies. But any future plans came to a sudden halt on November 9, 1922. A tragic accident shaped the remaining years of her life. On November 2, Oakley, Frank, and their dog, Dave, boarded a boat for Florida. They planned to spend the winter with some friends there. In Jacksonville, they put Dave on a train and traveled on by automobile, planning to meet up with the pooch in Leesburg. On November 9, a chauffeur was driving their Cadillac on the Dixie Highway, about 46 miles (74 km) north of Daytona. As he tried to pass another car, he lost control. The vehicle flipped over an embankment, throwing Oakley from the car and pinning her beneath it. She was trapped under the weight of the Cadillac, suffering from a fractured hip and ankle. A passing car

The Rifle Queen

The Wild West was often a theme in dime novels. These short fiction stories were popular in the late 1800s and early 1900s. In 1887, Oakley's life and legend became the basis of *The Rifle Queen*. This 64-page novel claimed to be the "truthful and stirring story" of her life. However, there was little fact in the book, which cost just two pennies. The story portrayed Oakley as a girl who had grown up in Kansas. As a child, she had many adventures. She put a bullet through the eye of a panther and killed an evil villain. In one part of the book, she shot a wolf. When she opened the jaws to skin it, she suddenly discovered that the wolf was still alive. The beast's jaws clamped down tightly on her arm, but according to the story, she never even cried out in pain. *The Rifle Queen* must have been an amusing read for Oakley. She learned that she had even killed a bear, survived a raging blizzard, and saved a train from a band of robbers.

stopped, and the man inside helped Oakley out from under the car and drove her to a Daytona hospital.

Butler escaped the accident uninjured. He hurried to Leesburg, picked up Dave, and brought the dog back to Daytona so they could all be together. For the next six weeks, Butler and Dave stayed in an apartment across the street from the hospital. They both visited Oakley every day. Butler later wrote a touching story about those weeks from Dave's point of view. The story, titled *The Life of Dave, As Told by Himself*, was later printed in a Newark, New Jersey, newspaper.

Things went from bad to worse. In February 1923, as Oakley recovered in Leesburg, Butler took Dave out for a walk. While they were heading back to the hotel, Dave spotted a squirrel and chased after it. He ran into the street and was hit by a passing car. He was killed instantly. For 10 years, Dave had been a part of the family. Now suddenly, he was gone, leaving Oakley and Butler heartbroken.

By spring, Oakley was finally back on her feet again with the help of crutches. She agreed to do an exhibition at Cooke Field in Leesburg, where the Philadelphia Phillies baseball team held their spring training. Oakley had not fired a gun since October 8, 1922. "Still I think my eye is good and maybe I'll be able to shoot fairly straight," she said. Like always, Butler set up her table of shotguns and rifles, and Oakley hobbled out onto the baseball diamond. There, she dropped her crutches and leaned her full weight onto her good left leg.

Oakley was right about her aim—it was as sharp as ever. She pinged pennies and sent them whizzing across the field. She tossed eggs in the air and shot a bullet through them before they hit the dirt. After she finished her stunts, a group of young boys who had gathered in the stands scurried onto the field to pick up the pennies she had shot. The Phillies players applauded and cheered.

That summer, Oakley's injuries continued to heal, and she hoped that, one day, she would be as strong as she had been before the accident. She recalled illnesses from her younger days. "Why, I have been told three different times by various doctors that I would never get on a horse again!" she reminded her friends. "But I always did!" This time, however, would prove different. Oakley finally went from crutches to a cane, but she was forced to wear a leg brace for the rest of her life.

"AIM AT
A HIGH MARK"

By 1924, Annie Oakley began to develop anemia, a condition that keeps the blood from carrying enough oxygen throughout the body. Without proper oxygen, organs and tissues slowly deteriorate. The most common symptoms of anemia, which is sometimes caused by an iron or vitamin deficiency, are paleness and fatigue. Oakley could feel her body growing weak and tired. Yet, she remained cheerful and refused to complain.

Oakley's illness caused her to look back on her life. By persevering through a difficult childhood, she had learned that a person could achieve anything if she only kept trying. She wrote a motto that captured this belief and had it copyrighted by the Elliott Service Company of New York. "Aim at a high mark, and you'll hit it," she wrote. "No, not the first time, nor the second time and maybe not the third. But keep on aiming and keep on shooting, for only practice will make you perfect. Finally, you'll hit the bull's eye of success."

Realizing her health was failing, Oakley decided she wanted to go home, but not to Maryland. She wanted to spend her final years in the countryside she knew as a child, near the fields and forests she trampled through so long ago. In December 1924, she and Butler arrived in Dayton, Ohio. A few months later, they bought a large,

Annie Oakley continued to set shooting records in her sixties, even after her car accident. Despite her declining health, Oakley and her husband continued to quail hunt.

two-story white house with a front porch. Oakley's life as a traveling exhibition shooter was over, but the need to hold a gun never left her. Some afternoons, Oakley and Butler would go to the local trapshooting grounds, and she would do some shooting. Even as feeble as her body had become, the heavy gun did not waver in the least when she lifted it.

Sensing that their days were numbered, Butler and Oakley wrote their wills in the fall of 1925. During the winter of 1926, Oakley started to write an autobiography of her life, but she would not live to see it published. In April 1926, Oakley became so weak she

Annie Get Your Gun

"Anything you can do,
I can do better.
I can do anything
Better than you."

Those lyrics are from "Anything You Can Do," a rousing duet sung by the characters of Annie Oakley and Frank Butler in the hit Broadway musical *Annie Get Your Gun.* The song sets the scene for a climactic shooting

(continues)

To this day, Annie Oakley's spirit lives on in books, film, television, and plays. In 1999, *Annie Get Your Gun*, the Broadway musical based on Oakley's life, won the Tony Award for Best Revival of a Musical.

(continued)

contest between the two. Through *Annie Get Your Gun*, a highly fictional-
ized account of Oakley and Butler's courtship, the spirit of Oakley lives on
in popular culture. Another well-known standard from the musical is the
tune "There's No Business Like Show Business."

The musical first appeared on Broadway from May 1946 to February
1949 and starred Broadway legend Ethel Merman as Oakley. A revival ran
from 1999 to 2001, with Bernadette Peters playing Oakley. Later during the
run, country singer Reba McEntire took on the role of Oakley. In 1950, a
film version of the musical was produced, with Betty Hutton as Oakley.

had trouble getting out of bed. The Cherokee cowboy Will Rogers
happened to be in Dayton that month and paid Oakley a visit. He
was so touched by her frail health that he wrote a special article for
his daily column, which was published in nearly 200 newspapers
across the country each week. His column celebrated Annie Oakley's life and career, stating that she was "the greatest woman rifle
shot the world has ever produced." He then went on to tell Americans about her declining health. He encouraged people to write her
letters and visit her.

After the article was printed, Oakley received thousands of let-
ters from fans she had inspired over the years. They offered their
best wishes and prayers for a quick recovery, but it was not to be.
Before long, she needed constant care, and Butler could not handle
it alone. Now in his mid-seventies, Butler also had health problems.
They went to live with her niece, Bonnie Blakeley, in Darke County.
That fall, Butler hoped to take Oakley to Pinehurst for the winter.
Too weak to travel, she urged him to go alone. Butler decided to take
Oakley's niece, Fern, with him instead. He traveled to her home in
Detroit, Michigan, and they planned to head south from there. But
their travel plans were delayed when Butler became ill. Both Oakley
and Butler lay weak and bedridden, miles apart from each other for
the first time in years.

GOING HOME

Meanwhile, Oakley continued to get worse. In October, she asked to be taken to a home in Greenville where she could be close to her doctor. Knowing the end was near, she made her funeral requests. Always a modest and proper lady, Oakley wanted her body to be handled by another woman, not a man. For her funeral, she had selected an apricot-colored dress of georgette silk. After the funeral, Oakley wanted to be cremated.

On November 3, 1926, at 11:00 that night, 66-year-old Annie Oakley died in her sleep. Her doctor recorded the cause of death to be pernicious anemia. Some people believe, however, that she perhaps died of lead poisoning caused by years of handling guns and lead bullets. The next day, newspapers across the country ran this story: "In the hills of Darke County, Ohio, where the girl, Annie Oakley, learned to handle a rifle, will rest the ashes of the noted marksman, who was perhaps the greatest shooter of all time.... She was the friend of monarchs and the confidante of Sitting Bull."

On November 5, a private funeral service was held in Greenville, at the home of family friends. Oakley's family purposely told reporters that her funeral was to be held the following day. They did not want any disruptions from the curious public. After the service, Oakley's body was cremated, and the ashes were placed in a silver trophy cup given to her by the French. Before her death, Oakley had requested that the trophy cup be made into an urn, with a screw-on top.

In Michigan, the news of Oakley's death left Butler devastated. According to Fern, "He never ate a bite after she went." He had once told a friend that, if Oakley died before he did, he would be helpless. Utterly distraught, Butler did not last long. On November 21, 1926, just 18 days after Oakley passed, Butler died at Fern's home. His body was brought back to Darke County, and he was reunited with his wife. On November 25, they were buried side-by-side at Brock Cemetery near Greenville, Ohio.

Although Annie Oakley had died, her legend would live on. Her story has inspired Americans throughout the years. Numerous books and movies have highlighted her life and career. For many women, she became a symbol of independence and strength. Yet, all the while, she held firm to her belief in being a respectable lady. Many fans and admirers have stated that there was only one Annie Oakley, and there will never be another one like her.

CHRONOLOGY

1860   On August 13, Phoebe Ann (Annie) Moses is born in Darke County, Ohio, to Jacob and Susan Moses.

1866   Jacob Moses dies of pneumonia, throwing the family into financial despair.

1867   Mary Jane Moses, Annie's oldest sister, dies of tuberculosis; the Moses family moves to a smaller farm; wanting to help out, Annie starts to hunt quail and grouse in the surrounding woods.

1870   Susan sends Annie to a poor farm near Greenville, Ohio; Annie is sent to work for a cruel family she calls "the Wolves."

1872   Annie runs away from "the Wolves;" she goes to live with family friends Samuel and Nancy Edington; she learns to sew and embroider.

1875   Susan asks Annie to come back home; Annie begins to sell the game she shoots to the Katzenberger brothers' grocery store; she earns enough money to pay off her mother's mortgage.

1881   Annie beats famous marksman Frank Butler in a shooting match.

1882   Annie marries Butler on June 20; she replaces Butler's stage partner and starts doing her own shooting stunts as part of the act; she takes the stage name Annie Oakley.

1884   In March, Oakley meets Sitting Bull, who informally adopts her and gives her the name "Little Sure Shot;" in April, Butler and Oakley go on tour with the Sells Brothers' Circus.

1885   Oakley joins Buffalo Bill's Wild West show in April.

1887   The Wild West performs at the American Exposition in London, England; Oakley quits the Wild West in October and sails back to the United States.

TIMELINE

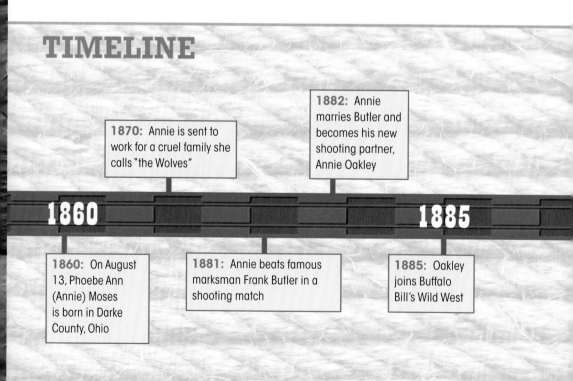

1870: Annie is sent to work for a cruel family she calls "the Wolves"

1882: Annie marries Butler and becomes his new shooting partner, Annie Oakley

1860

1885

1860: On August 13, Phoebe Ann (Annie) Moses is born in Darke County, Ohio

1881: Annie beats famous marksman Frank Butler in a shooting match

1885: Oakley joins Buffalo Bill's Wild West

1888   After a month with Pawnee Bill's show, Annie stars in her own play—*Deadwood Dick: Or the Sunbeam of the Sierras.*

1889   Oakley rejoins the Wild West and travels with the show to Paris for the Universal Exposition; the Wild West goes on a three-year tour of Europe.

1893   Oakley and Butler move into a new home in Nutley, New Jersey.

1901   During a spa treatment in Hot Springs, Arkansas, Oakley suffers injuries from prolonged exposure to scalding water, and her hair turns white; her youthful image shattered, she quits the Wild West.

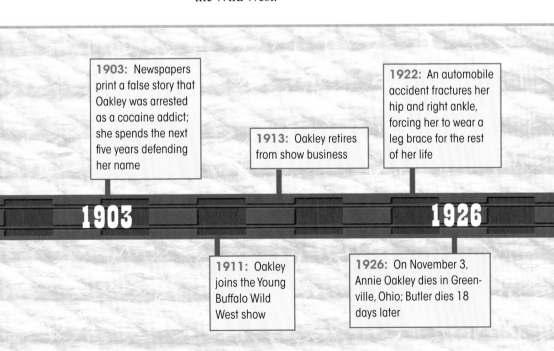

1903: Newspapers print a false story that Oakley was arrested as a cocaine addict; she spends the next five years defending her name

1913: Oakley retires from show business

1922: An automobile accident fractures her hip and right ankle, forcing her to wear a leg brace for the rest of her life

1903

1926

1911: Oakley joins the Young Buffalo Wild West show

1926: On November 3, Annie Oakley dies in Greenville, Ohio; Butler dies 18 days later

1902   Oakley stars in a stage play called *The Western Girl*.

1903   Newspapers across the country print a false story that Oakley was arrested as a cocaine addict; she spends the next five-plus years defending her name.

1910   Oakley makes a guest appearance at the Wild West show; Buffalo Bill asks her to return to the show, but Oakley declines the offer.

1911   Oakley joins the Young Buffalo Wild West show.

1913   Oakley retires from show business.

1917   In April, the United States enters World War I; Oakley visits soldiers in training camps.

1918   World War I ends on November 11; Oakley celebrates by giving a show in Pinehurst, North Carolina.

1922   Oakley and Butler get into an automobile accident on the Dixie Highway in Florida; Oakley fractures her hip and right ankle, forcing her to wear a leg brace for the rest of her life.

1924   Oakley and Butler move to Dayton, Ohio.

1926   On November 3, Annie Oakley dies in Greenville, Ohio, at age 66; Butler dies 18 days later on November 21.

GLOSSARY

anemia A condition in which the blood is deficient in red blood cells.

black powder Also known as gunpowder, black powder is made of saltpeter, charcoal, and sulfur. It burns quickly and is used in fireworks and was formerly used in firearms.

buckshot Small lead pellets used in shotgun shells.

burlesque A theater show that often involves stripping.

bustle A pad or framework that expands and supports the fullness of a back of a woman's skirt or dress.

cartridge A case containing an explosive charge for blasting.

chauffeur Someone who drives a car for someone else.

coronation A ceremony in which a person is crowned.

darning Mending a hole in cloth.

frostbite The superficial or deep freezing of the tissues of some part of the body.

gondola A long, narrow, flat-bottomed boat used on the canals of Venice, Italy.

knickerbockers Loose-fitting short pants gathered at the knee.

nomadic Roams from place to place.

pantaloon A type of knee-length pants; also, a buffoon in pantomime shows.

pantomime   A skit done without words.

percussion cap   A thin, metal cap that contains an explosive substance.

radical   Something that departs from the norm; an unusual or extreme idea.

ration   A limited portion of food.

regiment   A military unit.

sanatorium   An institution for treating chronic diseases.

shot   Like buckshot, tiny lead balls used in gun shells.

sidesaddle   A saddle in which the rider sits with both legs on one side of the horse.

tuberculosis   A deadly lung disease.

uprising   When a group rebels against another group with violence.

BIBLIOGRAPHY

Annie Oakley: American Experience Series. PBS Video, 2006.

Annie Oakley Biography. Buffalo Bill Historical Center. Available online at http://www.bbhc.org/bbm/biographyAO.cfm.

"Annie Oakley: The American Experience." PBS.com. Available online at http://www.pbs.org/wgbh/amex/oakley.

Brown, Dee. *The Wild West.* New York: Warner Books, 1993.

Havighurst, Walter. *Annie Oakley of the Wild West.* New York: MacMillan Co., 1954.

Kasper, Shirl. *Annie Oakley.* Norman, Okla.: University of Oklahoma Press, 1992.

McMurtry, Larry. *The Colonel and Little Missie: Buffalo Bill, Annie Oakley, and the Beginnings of Superstardom in America.* New York: Simon & Schuster, 2005.

Riley, Glenda. *The Life and Legacy of Annie Oakley.* Norman, Okla.: University of Oklahoma Press, 1994.

Stegner, Page. *Winning the Wild West: The Epic Saga of the American Frontier: 1800–1899.* New York: The Free Press, 2002.

FURTHER RESOURCES

Bloom, Barbara Lee. *Nat Love*. New York: Chelsea House, 2010.

Brown, Dee. *The Gentle Tamers: Women of the Old Wild West*. Lincoln, Neb.: Bison Books, 1981.

Enss, Chris. *Buffalo Gals: Women of Buffalo Bill's Wild West Show*. Guilford, Conn.: TwoDot, 2005.

Flood, Elizabeth Clair. *Cowgirls: Women of the Wild West*. Santa Fe, N.M.: Zon International Publishing, 2000.

Hasday, Judy L. *Davy Crockett*. New York: Chelsea House, 2010.

Macy, Sue. *Bull's-Eye: A Photobiography of Annie Oakley*. Washington, D.C.: National Geographic Children's Books, 2006.

Reis, Ronald A. *Sitting Bull*. New York: Chelsea House, 2010.

Riley, Glenda, and Richard Etulain, editors. *Wild Women of the Old West*. Golden, Colo.: Fulcrum Publishing, 2003.

Woog, Adam. *Jesse James*. New York: Chelsea House, 2010.

———. *Wyatt Earp*. New York: Chelsea House, 2010.

Film/DVD

Annie Oakley. Turner Home Entertainment, 1935.

Annie Oakley (4-DVD set). Echo Bridge Home Entertainment, 2008.

Annie Oakley: American Experience Series. PBS Video, 2006.

Annie Oakley: Crackshot in Petticoats. A&E Home Video, 2006.

Shelley Duvall's Tall Tales and Legends: Annie Oakley. Koch Vision, 2005.

Web Sites

Annie Oakley Days Festival

http://www.annieoakleyfestival.org/

This three-day event has been held for the past 45 years in Greenville, Ohio. The people of Greenville celebrate the life of Annie Oakley with a parade, a shooting contest, a photography and art show, a karaoke contest, and an Annie Oakley impersonator.

Buffalo Bill Historical Center

http://www.bbhc.org/home

Located in northwestern Wyoming, near Yellowstone National Park's East Gate, the Buffalo Bill Historical Center is regarded by many as the finest Western museum in the country.

PBS American Experience: Annie Oakley

http://www.pbs.org/wgbh/amex/oakley

This site is the online companion to the PBS biography about Annie Oakley. Features color and black and white images, a teacher's guide, virtual tours, and program interviews.

The Wild West

http://www.thewildwest.org/cowboys-western

This comprehensive site features biographies, history, and lore about the Wild West. Includes legendary women, American Indians, cowboys, poetry, recipes, and historical and modern information.

PICTURE CREDITS

Page

INDEX

ABOUT THE AUTHOR

Rachel A. Koestler-Grack has worked with nonfiction books as an editor and writer since 1999. During her career, she has worked extensively with historical topics, ranging from the Middle Ages to the colonial era to the civil rights movement. In addition, she has written numerous biographies on a variety of historical and contemporary figures. Rachel lives with her husband and daughter in the German community of New Ulm, Minnesota.